W9-AWZ-440

GEORGIA ICONS

GEORGIA ICONS

50 CLASSIC VIEWS
OF THE PEACH STATE

Don Rhodes

with photographs by *Jeff Barnes*

gpp

Guilford, Connecticut

Project editor: David Legere
Text design: Casey Shain

Photos by Jeff Barnes.

Library of Congress Cataloging-in-Publication Data is available on file.

ISBN 978-0-7627-6072-5

Printed in China

10 9 8 7 6 5 4 3 2 1

CONTENTS

Acknowledgments..viii

Introduction ix

Apples 2

Baseball in Georgia 4

Brer Rabbit 6

James Brown 8

Archie Butt's *Titanic* Bridge......................10

Cathedral of St. John the Baptist.........12

Ray Charles..14

Claxton Fruitcake...16

Coastal Islands 18

Ty Cobb..20

Coca-Cola...22

Cotton Is King!...24

Historic Douglass Theatre.........................26

Elberton's Stonehenge 28

FDR's Little White House............................30

Filming in Georgia.......................................32

Forsyth Park Fountain 34

Georgia-Inspired Songs 36

Georgia's Capital before Atlanta...........38

Gold-Domed Capitol 40

Golfing on Historic Courses......................42

Governors' Mansions 44

Jekyll Island:
The Millionaires' Playground...................46

Juliette Gordon Low 48

Martha Berry College...................................50

Mother Church of Civil Rights 52

Ocmulgee Indian Mounds 54

Flannery O'Connor's Andalusia 56

Peach-Pickin' Time Down in Georgia .. 58

Peanuts in the Peach State 60

Providence Canyon
and Other Natural Wonders 62

The Real Garden of Good and Evil 64

Recycling Old Georgia Buildings 66

Otis Redding 68

Rivers of Georgia 70

Rock Eagle Effigy 72

Roses in Thomasville 74

Cherokee Chief John Ross 76

Savannah's St. Patrick's Day Parade ... 78

Savannah's Waving Girl 80

Seeds from the Sower 82

Springer Opera House 84

Stone Mountain 86

Swampwise Okefenokee Joe 88

Tybee Lighthouse 90

The Varsity: World's
Largest Drive-In Restaurant 92

World-Famous Vidalia Onions 94

Beautiful and Dangerous Waterfalls 96

Watson Mill Covered Bridge 98

White-Columned Mansions 100

About the Author/Photographer 102

ACKNOWLEDGMENTS

I would first like to thank my life partner and closest friend, Ervin Edward "Eddie" Smith Jr., for his support, along with our great four-legged companions, Rusty, Willard, and Jayme Brown.

I'd also like to thank Erin Turner, senior editor of Globe Pequot Press, and the editorial board of GPP. Thanks also to Amy Alexander and Bob Sembiante at GPP, as well as the project editor, David Legere, text designer, Casey Shain, and copyeditor, Melissa J. Hayes.

And, in no particular order, my gratefulness goes out to my father, Ollen Columbus Rhodes, and his wife, Jean Swann; my sisters, Linda Groover and her husband, Sammy; Ann Holland and her husband, George; and Jan Harris and her husband, Jerry Jarriel; my brothers, Larry Rhodes and his wife, Teresa; Mike Spence and his wife, Kathy; and Doug Spence and his wife, Bobbi, for their support; as well as my late mother, Ella Sampert Rhodes, who gave me my love of reading and music.

Thanks to those who supported me during the writing process: my friends Pat Claiborne, Johnny Edwards, Flo Carter, Jim Taylor at Ohio University in Zanesville, Reverend Dan White, Free Pennington, Dave Hunt, David Hobbs, photographer Jeff Barnes, and Bill and Linda Macky, for listening to my stories as I researched this book.

And thanks especially to my friends at Morris Communications and *The Augusta Chronicle:* Kay Pruitt, Billy and Will Morris, Martha Jean McHaney, Tharon Giddens, Bill Kirby, Don Bailey, Mark Albertin, Sherry Fulmer, and Pete May.

Finally, thanks to God for all the great friends and family members who continue to enrich my life. I'm so blessed.

—DON RHODES, AUTHOR

Thanks to my wife, Tonya Rowland; Joy Forth at the Governor's Mansion in Atlanta; Marti Pirkle at Stone Mountain Park in Stone Mountain; Eric Little of the Augusta GreenJackets baseball team in Augusta; Michelle Keener at Michelle's Sweet Creations in Lakemont; Neil Ghingold of Neil Ghingold Antiques in Augusta; Marcia Campbell at the Robert Toombs House in Washington; staff employees for their help at the Springer Opera House in Columbus; Douglass Theatre in Macon; Southeastern Natural Sciences Academy at Phinizy Swamp in Augusta; Flannery O'Connor's Andalusia home in Milledgeville; Little White House in Warm Springs; and Eryn Eubanks.

—JEFF BARNES, PHOTOGRAPHER

INTRODUCTION

When I began telling people about my fourth national and international book for Globe Pequot Press, the question most often asked has been: Is this about people who are icons?

Yes, I would explain, extremely famous people *can* be icons, but so are places and things that are objects of great devotion—objects that are so familiar they represent something special to the viewer.

The great photographs in this book were taken by professional photographer (and award-winning Elvis Presley tribute artist) Jeff Barnes, who is based in Evans, Georgia. He has captured iconic representations of people, places, and things that have a lot of meaning, especially for Georgians.

Although Jeff has lived in Georgia for many years and was a staff photographer for *The Augusta Chronicle* and, later, Morris Communications, he grew up on the Outer Banks of North Carolina and really knew very little about the state of Georgia until he started working on this book.

I grew envious as he crisscrossed the huge state, calling me on his cell phone from the Ray Charles statue in Albany, the governor's mansion in Atlanta, Martha Berry College in Rome, Springer Opera House in Columbus, Martin Luther King Jr.'s Ebenezer Baptist Church in Atlanta, the Ocmulgee Indian Mounds near Macon, FDR's Little White House in Warm Springs, and so forth, all excited about some wonderful thing he had just seen.

One of the strangest calls I've ever received came from the real garden of good and evil (Bonaventure Cemetery) in Savannah, when Jeff called to double-check on which gravestone I wanted photographed. I think that's the only call I've ever had from a cemetery.

His photographic excursions and my editorial research have been combined into this coffee-table book full of beautiful color photos, useful Web site addresses, and unusual bits and pieces of Georgia history.

Georgia was founded as a colony in 1733 by British general James Edward Oglethorpe and became the fourth state to ratify the United States Constitution in 1788. Its early inhabitants included many Native American tribes, as well as Spanish, French, German, and Swiss explorers and settlers.

There have been many books about Georgia and its rich history, colorful and talented people, industrial and agricultural contributions, resort areas, tourist destinations, and geographical diversity.

I sincerely hope this one will provide readers and viewers with an even greater knowledge and appreciation of the state that I have loved for so many years and that is always on my mind.

GEORGIA ICONS

APPLES

Cornelia in north Georgia is noted for many things: It is the area where baseball legend Ty Cobb spent the last three years of his life, not far from where he was born; it's where the Walt Disney Company filmed its popular 1956 movie, *The Great Locomotive Chase*; and it's the site of the supposed last train holdup in Georgia.

And, oh yes, it's also the home of the "Big Red Apple."

The citizens of Cornelia and Habersham County were so grateful that apple trees saved them from economic ruin after the boll weevil destroyed their cotton crops, they erected the Big Red Apple downtown, in 1925.

The apple itself weighs 5,200 pounds and is 7 feet tall and 22 feet around. It was constructed of steel and concrete in Winchester, Virginia, and erected on a concrete pedestal that stands 8 feet high and 6 feet square at the base. It was the community project of the then-new Kiwanis Club and was donated to the city and county by the Southern Railway. Among those at its dedication on June 4, 1926, was U.S. senator Walter F. George.

For more information about Georgia's apple industry, visit georgiaapplefestival.org and corneliageorgia.org.

Apples are now big business in north Georgia. There are about 360,000 apple-bearing trees in the state, with Georgia farmers producing about ten billion (!) pounds of apples annually, according to the Georgia Department of Agriculture.

The harvest season is from about late July into December. Popular varieties grown include Ozark Gold, Paulard, Red Delicious, Golden Delicious, Rome Beauty, Mutzu Crispin, Empire, Jonagold, Jonathan, Arkansas Black, Fuji, Granny Smith, Stayman Winesap, and Yates.

During the first weekend of October, Cornelia merchants and civic clubs host the Big Red Apple Festival, featuring crafts, specialty foods, all kinds of entertainment, an antique car show, and the Big Red Apple 5K Run.

Nearby Ellijay in Gilmer County has its own "Georgia Apple Festival" the second and third weekends of October at the Ellijay Lions Club Fairground.

Thousands of visitors converge on those two cities each October to eat apple pies, drink apple juice, and celebrate one of Georgia's sturdiest and best cash crops.

BASEBALL IN GEORGIA

Baseball was being played in Georgia in the 1800s, but it was the formation of the South Atlantic League in November of 1903 that really gave the game a huge boost in popularity.

The SALLY League, as it was also known, consisted of six teams in the cities of Macon, Augusta, and Savannah, Georgia; Columbia and Charleston, South Carolina; and Jacksonville, Florida, with the league's first games played on the same day in April of 1904.

The creation of that league also gave the game its greatest player, Tyrus Raymond Cobb, who was born on a farm outside Cornelia, Georgia, and who lived from ages five to seventeen in Royston, Georgia. Cobb wrote to all six SALLY league teams but only the Augusta Tourists offered him a chance to play.

It was Cobb's good fortune that at this same time, the major-league teams in Boston, Philadelphia, New York, and Detroit were using Augusta for spring training and often played against the Tourists, who of course usually lost. But it gave Detroit manager Bill Armour a chance to see the teenage baseball wonder up close.

The Georgia Sports Hall of Fame (gshf.org) in Macon is a good place to start learning about the state's baseball heroes. The official Web site for the Atlanta Braves is atlanta.braves.mlb.com.

Cobb played his last game as a member of the Augusta Tourists on August 25, 1905, and played his first game as a member of the Detroit Tigers less than a week later, on August 30.

Major-league baseball took a giant leap in Georgia when the Milwaukee Braves moved to Atlanta. That led to the construction of the $18 million Atlanta Stadium with its 52,769 seats, completed in the spring of 1965. That summer the stadium would host the only Georgia appearance of the Beatles. Barbra Streisand would follow with her own concert there during the summer of 1966.

The stadium's name evolved into the Atlanta-Fulton County Stadium. This facility lasted until the construction of the 85,000-seat Centennial Olympic Stadium, in order for Atlanta to host the 1996 Summer Olympic Games. The stadium was remodeled to accommodate the Braves, with the Atlanta-Fulton County Stadium demolished to make way for more parking spaces.

Since the remodeled stadium was leased to then Braves owner and media giant Ted Turner, this led to the stadium being renamed Turner Field.

BRER RABBIT

One of the most unusual statues in Georgia is that of a rabbit standing erect on his hind legs on the courthouse square in Eatonton. Popularized by newspaper journalist, novelist, and folklorist Joel Chandler Harris, Brer Rabbit is no ordinary hare; along with Warner Brothers' Bugs Bunny and Beatrix Potter's Peter Rabbit, he is one of the most famous rabbits in the world.

Harris was honored by U.S. president Theodore Roosevelt at the White House, and was named to the American Academy of Arts and Letters. He wrote more than 180 Uncle Remus and Brer Rabbit stories, inspired by his early life working on Southern plantations and told in the dialect of African-American slaves. The stories are both praised by folklore experts for their creativity and severely criticized by black and white civil rights leaders, for portraying a fictionalized, idyllic relationship between black slaves and their white owners.

Fellow Eatonton novelist Alice Walker (*The Color Purple*) once wrote that Harris had stolen her African-American folklore heritage and had

The Brer Rabbit statue is located on the Putnam County Courthouse grounds in downtown Eatonton; visit wrensnestonline .com for more information about author Joel Chandler Harris.

made it a white man's publishing commodity. The name "Uncle Remus" also has become a derogatory characterization of a black person who goes along with white politicians or business leaders just to get in good with them.

Nevertheless, Harris's writings remain an important part of Southern literature. His former home, The Wren's Nest, is located at 1050 Ralph David Abernathy Boulevard S.W. in Atlanta, just off Interstate 20, and is on the National Register of Historic Places.

The 1946 Walt Disney movie, *Song of the South,* is based on Harris's characters. The film is a collector's item among movie buffs, even though the Disney corporation, at this writing, still has not released it on DVD. Most movie buffs are unaware that James Baskett, the actor who portrayed Uncle Remus and sang "Zip-A-Dee-Doo-Dah" in the movie, actually was born in Indiana.

In addition to his amazing literary output of articles and books, Harris also served as associate editor of both the *Savannah Morning News* and the *Atlanta Journal-Constitution.*

JAMES BROWN

One day in 2004, then-mayor of Augusta Bob Young called yours truly and asked if I would write the inscription for the metal plaque that would be placed on a brick pedestal near the statue of world-famous entertainer James Brown.

The statue now stands in the middle of Broad Street in the 800 block, across from the Augusta Common park, with a plaque bearing these words:

> Singer, songwriter, musician and one-of-a-kind performer James Brown has thrilled millions around the world with his hit recordings and electrifying performances. The 1983 Georgia Music Hall of Fame inductee, 1986 Rock and Roll Hall of Fame inductee and 2003 Kennedy Center honoree has called Augusta "home" since moving here when he was five. It was in Augusta's Lenox Theater that he first received recognition for his talent by winning an amateur contest. His songs have enriched the world, and his personality and generosity have enriched this city.

Brown's family, lifelong friends, and business associates were present on November 15, 2003, when a ceremony

If you forget your camera when you visit the James Brown statue in Augusta, no problem; you can visit www .augustaarts.com /jamesbrowncam .htm. And to learn more about James Brown, read the bio Say It Loud! My Memories of James Brown, Soul Brother No. 1.

was held to unveil the clay model for the statue on the Augusta Common. The statue was to be sculpted by Augusta orthopedic surgeon Dr. John Savage. When the clay figure was revealed—standing erect, with a big, floor-length cape, a huge shock of hair, and its left hand clasped to its chest, holding a microphone—Brown proclaimed, "Looks like Thomas Jefferson! Looks like Thomas Jefferson!" Sure enough, the clay model really did resemble the Jefferson Memorial in Washington, D.C.

Brown himself would unveil the completed $40,000 statue in a ceremony on May 6, 2005. The keynote speaker was Brown's former road manager, Reverend Al Sharpton, who urged the crowd to sing "Happy Birthday" to Brown (he had turned seventy-two just three days earlier).

"This is not a statue for his ego," Sharpton said. "This is a statue to give young people hope all over the world."

The soul music legend, who died on Christmas Day in 2006, was very proud of the statue and often took people to see it.

ARCHIE BUTT'S *TITANIC* BRIDGE

On Monday, April 15, 1912, Augustans woke up to read this headline on the front page of *The Augusta Chronicle:*

LINER TITANIC HIT AN ICEBERG

THE LARGEST VESSEL AFLOAT REPORTED BY WIRELESS TO HAVE BEEN IN COLLISION ON HER MAIDEN VOYAGE CARRIED THIRTEEN HUNDRED PASSENGERS— MAJOR ARCHIE BUTT AMONG THOSE ON BOARD—LEFT SOUTHAMPTON APRIL 10 FOR NEW YORK

Many *Chronicle* readers knew and loved Archibald Willingham Butt, who had been born and reared in their city and who had achieved international fame as the military aide and trusted friend of two United States presidents.

Within days of the ocean liner's sinking on April 12, 1912, proposals were made to create a memorial to Butt, and, within a brief time, funds were raised to construct the Butt Memorial Bridge, which exists today on Fifteenth Street over the Augusta Canal.

Butt worked as a newspaper reporter for daily newspapers in Louisville, Kentucky, and Macon, Georgia, before becoming a correspondent in the nation's capital for several southern

Butt Memorial Bridge is located over the Augusta Canal on Fifteenth Street; for more information, visit www .titanic-titanic .com/titanic_ memorials.shtml and also http:// en.wikipedia .org/wiki/ Archibald_Butt.

newspapers. He joined the United States Army during the Spanish-American War and eventually became the military aide to U.S. presidents Theodore Roosevelt and William Howard Taft.

By late March of 1912, Butt was in Rome, Italy, on a trip to improve his health. He not only had a private audience with King Victor Emmanuel, but also reportedly with Pope Pius X. Then, for his return trip to the States, he made a fatal decision: He bought a ticket for the maiden Atlantic crossing of the *Titanic,* which he boarded April 10 at Southampton, England. He was last seen helping women and children into lifeboats. His remains were never recovered.

President Taft was present on May 2, 1912, for Butt's memorial service, held in the Grand Opera House in Augusta, and, after his presidency, Taft returned to Augusta on April 15, 1914, for the dedication of the Butt Memorial Bridge, honoring his late friend.

The bridge is thought to be the only *Titanic* memorial in the state of Georgia, and the only bridge in the world dedicated to a victim of the oceanic tragedy.

CATHEDRAL OF
ST. JOHN THE BAPTIST

Every St. Patrick's Day in Savannah begins with a mass at the twin-spire Cathedral of St. John the Baptist, which serves as the "mother church" of the Catholic Diocese of Savannah. The diocese consists of more than 73,000 Catholics in fifty-four parishes and twenty-five missions throughout the southern half of the state.

At the 2010 St. Patrick's Day Mass, more than one thousand people packed every pew to hear the Most Reverend J. Kevin Boland, thirteenth bishop of Savannah, preside over the ninety-minute-long worship service, paying tribute to the Catholic saint, Patrick.

Upon seeing the Cathedral of St. John the Baptist for the first time, visitors usually use words like "awesome," "beautiful," "majestic," and "incredible."

Its history goes back to when French Catholics, fleeing the slave uprisings on Haiti and Santo Domingo in the late eighteenth century, established Savannah's first parish, which they called the Congrégation de Saint Jean-Baptiste.

Bishop John England placed the cornerstone of the new church in 1835,

You can take a virtual tour of the cathedral and learn about visitation times at savannah cathedral.org.

between Perry and McDonough Streets. In April of 1839, Bishop England dedicated the house of worship as the Church of Saint John the Baptist. The Right Reverend Thomas A. Becker, sixth bishop of Savannah, completed an expansion of a new brick cathedral building in 1896, with its lofty twin spires and French Gothic design.

Tragedy struck on February 6, 1898, when a fire gutted the cathedral, leaving only the outside walls and the two spires standing. The bishop's residence was spared.

It was Father Benjamin Keiley, seventh bishop of Savannah, who presided over the first mass celebrated in the rebuilt cathedral on Christmas Eve of 1899. Improvements and renovations to the cathedral continued to be made throughout the twentieth century.

In 1998, the Most Reverend J. Kevin Boland began a major restoration project, which involved the removal, cleaning, and re-leading of more than fifty stained-glass windows, replacement of the slate roof, and restoration of the interior.

RAY CHARLES

The city of Albany showed respect for its native son, Ray Charles Robinson, in December of 2007 by unveiling a large bronze statue in the middle of a $2 million downtown plaza that bears his name.

In 1978, Charles and record producer Bill Lowery became the first two inductees into the Georgia Music Hall of Fame.

Contrary to the 2004 film, *Ray,* starring Jamie Foxx, Charles was never "banned" from Georgia until the General Assembly invited him to perform his hit version of "Georgia on My Mind" in the state capitol, just before adopting it as the state song.

Here are the facts:

Ray Charles and his orchestra performed in Augusta's Bell Auditorium on October 15, 1957, along with Mickey & Sylvia, The Del Vikings, The Moonglows, Big Joe Turner, Roy Brown, Bo Diddley, and others.

Four years later, on March 15, 1961, Charles—by then a big star—was set to return to Bell Auditorium. But on the day of the show, he received a tele-

You can learn more about Ray Charles and other music artists from the Peach State at georgiamusic.org.

gram from Silas Norman Jr., president of the Paine College student body, and brother of future opera star, Jessye Norman, saying that the larger dance side of the auditorium would be reserved for whites, while blacks would have to sit in the smaller Music Hall side, which used the same stage.

Charles issued a statement saying he would not perform that night, and he left town. There was no incident other than the telegram, and he was not subsequently banned from the state. He was sued by the promoter and fined $757 in Fulton County Superior Court in Atlanta on June 14, 1962, and that was that. He was back in Bell Auditorium the following year with his backup group, the Raelettes.

Yours truly saw him perform in Atlanta in 1962, met him backstage at the University of Georgia's Coliseum in 1966, and was with him several times in Augusta in 1973—all before he supposedly was invited "to return" to the state and perform before the Georgia General Assembly in 1979.

Don't believe everything you see in the movies.

CLAXTON FRUITCAKE

One of the best things to happen to the small south-central Georgia town of Claxton was when Italian baker Savino Tos decided to put down roots in 1910.

While working in Macon, Georgia, for a company that made ice cream, the Italian immigrant noticed that Claxton did not have a bakery, so he started one, making his own Italian pastries, candy, and ice cream. His business continued to grow through the years.

In 1927, eleven-year-old Albert Parker was hired to sweep the floors. He began learning the bakery business and plunged into its daily operations. When company founder Tos decided to retire in 1945, he sold the company to Parker, who was smart enough to notice changing business patterns after World War II.

Parker saw that grocery stores and other outlets were competing for the bakery products and ice cream market, so he began reducing the Claxton Bakery product line, concentrating on fruitcake production. That first year of mass production, Parker and a handful of workers baked 45,000 pounds of Claxton Bakery fruitcakes.

Visitors can see the ovens of the Claxton Bakery from 8 a.m. to 5 p.m. Monday through Saturday (www.claxton fruitcake.com).

In the early 1950s, Parker was visited by a representative of the Civitan Club of Tampa, Florida, which was in search of an item to sell as part of their fund-raising efforts. That was the start of Claxton Bakery Inc., helping more than 1,000 organizations throughout North America to raise funds.

Albert Parker died on May 21, 1995, and his bakery was passed on to his three sons, Mid, Paul, and Dale, and his daughter, Betty. The company produces roughly five million pounds of fruitcake every year, with the peak baking season from September through December.

Besides Parker, Claxton Bakery founder Tos had another young apprentice named Ira Womble, who in 1948 opened the Georgia Fruitcake Company. His son, Ira Womble Jr., saw a need to furnish fruitcake to U.S. military servicemen and -women, and landed a contract to do just that.

Who would have thought that an Italian immigrant in the Old South would be responsible for Claxton, Georgia, becoming known as the Fruitcake Capital of the World?

COASTAL ISLANDS

Many people think the 1974 movie *Conrack,* based on Pat Conroy's first best-seller, *The Water Is Wide,* was filmed around Beaufort, South Carolina, since the cinematic versions of most of Conroy's books have been filmed in that area. However, the story of a young white teacher (Conroy, played by Jon Voight) who tries to instruct poorly educated black students on a desolate South Carolina island was actually filmed around coastal Brunswick and Darien, Georgia, and nearby St. Simons Island.

When people think of Georgia, they typically conjure up visions of cotton fields, magnolias, Spanish moss, and white-columned antebellum mansions; rarely do they think of shrimp boats and Georgia's several barrier islands. Among them is Cumberland Island, where John Fitzgerald Kennedy Jr. married Carolyn Bessette on September 21, 1996, in a tiny wooden church.

Another in the coastal chain is St. Simons, where Captain John Barry of the United States Navy in 1794 supervised the cutting and shipping of live oak timber for the construction of the battleship USS *Constitution,* affec-

The photo on the right shows shrimp boats in the morning light at Darien on the Georgia coast. More about Georgia's coastal islands can be found at http://www.visit coastalgeorgia .com.

tionately known as "Old Ironsides." It was also the setting of Eugenia Price's romance novels about the real-life Reverend Anson Dodge, and where Price herself was buried in 1996, at Christ Church Cemetery, not far from Dodge.

Sapelo Island, settled by French planters, was owned for many years by tobacco king R. J. Reynolds and Howard Coffin, chief engineer and executive of the Oldsmobile, Chalmers, and Hudson automobile companies.

AT&T president Theodore Vail was staying on Jekyll Island when he made the ceremonial first transcontinental phone call in 1915, connecting with President Woodrow Wilson in Washington, D.C., Alexander Graham Bell in New York, and Thomas Watson in San Francisco.

St. Catherine's Island was owned at one time by Creek Indian Mary Musgrove, interpreter and cultural advisor to Georgia founder, British general James Oglethorpe, and other colonists. After her death, the island was leased by Button Gwinnett, one of Georgia's three signers of the Declaration of Independence.

TY COBB

Following their 1908 marriage, Detroit Tigers baseball player Tyrus Raymond Cobb and his wife, the former Charlie Marion Lombard, lived off-seasons with her parents in their beautiful, two-story Victorian home south of Augusta. In 1913, Cobb moved his family into a two-story house at 2425 Williams Street. It exists today, a few blocks from the main entrance of Augusta State University.

There they raised daughter Shirley, born in Detroit, Michigan, and sons, Ty Jr., Herschel, and Jimmy, and daughter, Beverly, all born in Augusta.

Famous visitors to the Williams Street house ranged from patriotic band conductor John Philip Sousa to baseball commissioner Kenesaw Mountain Landis. Future television and movie star Dub Taylor, who lived nearby and was a friend of Ty Cobb Jr.'s, recalled spending nights in the Cobb home. It was in the Williams Street house that Cobb would hold press conferences and celebrations of his December birthday.

For more about Ty Cobb, visit www.tycobb museum.org, and read the bio, Ty Cobb: Safe at Home.

Cobb's youngest daughter, Beverly McLaren, remembers that the family loved animals, telling the author of this book:

> We had a lot of animals at the Williams Street house. My sister had a show horse. My brother, Jimmy, had a Shetland pony. We had a billy goat. My brother, Herschel, also had a nanny goat. My father had fifteen hunting dogs in a kennel there, and my mother had a canary bird. We also had two pigeons that got loose in the house one time. My younger brother and I also had rabbits.

McLaren also recalled that her father used a small room on the first floor as his office. Located just down the hall from the front entrance, the room featured a rolltop desk, and locked storage for his guns.

Cobb's oldest daughter, Shirley Beckworth, told this author that her father slept in a separate upstairs bedroom from her mother because he was a night owl. "I never saw his light off in his bedroom," she said. "He was always reading. He especially loved books about Napoleon and Julius Caesar."

COCA-COLA

By the 1800s, people had discovered that if they mixed water and carbonic gas, they could create an effervescent liquid that tasted like water from mineral springs. Joseph Hawkins in 1809 was granted the first United States patent to manufacture mineral waters.

Then, in 1886, pharmacist John S. Pemberton of Columbus, Georgia, came up with a blend of natural flavorings from all over the world and created a syrup which blended perfectly with the shop-created carbonated water. Pemberton placed his discovery on sale at Jacob's Pharmacy in Atlanta on May 8, 1886, for five cents a glass.

Apparently it was Pemberton's partner, Frank M. Robinson, who suggested the name "Coca-Cola," and who first wrote the name in a flowing typeface script as a possible advertising logo.

Pemberton sold the rights to his syrup creation at a low price. He died on August 16, 1888, not realizing how famous his product would become.

Within a year of Pemberton's death, full rights to the product had been

John Pemberton, who created the syrup for Coca-Cola, is buried in Linwood Cemetery in Columbus, Georgia. His gravestone reads ORIGINATOR OF COCA-COLA.

acquired by Asa G. Candler, a native of Villa Rica, Georgia, who had come to Atlanta with $1.50 in his pocket. The total cost of acquiring full rights, he estimated, was $2,300. He would make millions from the product before his own death in 1929.

It didn't take long for Coca-Cola to explode under Candler's guidance, with the first bottling done in 1894 by Joseph A. Biedenharn of Vicksburg, Mississippi. The first bottling plant was created in Chattanooga, Tennessee, in 1899, led by Benjamin F. Thomas and Joseph B. Whitehead of Chattanooga. The second bottling plant was established in Atlanta in 1900. Annual sales of Coca-Cola hit the million-gallon mark in 1904. Robert W. Woodruff would lead Coca-Cola to worldwide success after being elected president of the company in 1923.

Now, more than 100 years after pharmacist Pemberton came up with his special syrup, literally billions of people are familiar with the Georgia-created product and all of its many subsidiaries.

COTTON IS KING!

Many Americans are aware of Eli Whitney's role in developing a cotton gin machine, but few know about the role of another Georgia resident named Phineas Miller.

After the Revolutionary War, patriot hero Major General Nathanael Greene was granted a plantation north of Savannah called Mulberry Grove. Greene moved his family there in 1785, bringing with them their children's tutor, Phineas Miller.

Greene died at Mulberry Grove the next year, and the children's tutor became manager of the plantation. Miller and Greene's widow, Caty, fell in love and married on June 13, 1796, with George and Martha Washington as witnesses.

Meanwhile, Massachusetts native Eli Whitney graduated from Yale College in 1792 and sailed for South Carolina to work on another plantation near Mulberry Grove. He met Caty Greene aboard the ship, and she talked Whitney into coming to Mulberry Grove to work on his inventions.

Whitney saw that cotton growers needed a better way to clean cotton bolls

Georgiacotton commission.org is a good site for more information about the state's cotton industry. Just go to google .com and type Eli Whitney into the search window for many sites about the inventor.

of their seeds. At the time, it took a slave a full day to clean one pound of cotton. Within days, Whitney had created a design for his cotton gin, and by April of 1793, he had built one that cleaned fifty pounds a day. He and Phineas Miller became business partners the following month.

Whitney actually perfected his invention at a plantation Miller owned on Upton Creek near Washington, Georgia. It was there that Whitney "ginned" the first bale of cotton in the United States, and where, in 1810, the first cotton factory south of Massachusetts was built.

The Millers unfortunately fell upon hard times and had to sell Mulberry Grove.

Other plantation owners, however, became rich from growing cotton, with United States senator James Henry Hammond declaring in 1858, on the floor of the Senate, "What would happen if no cotton was furnished [by the South] for three years? . . . No, you dare not make war on cotton. . . . Cotton is king."

HISTORIC DOUGLASS THEATRE

Black theaters and churches in the racist South provided places where African Americans could forget their hardships while watching other black faces on movie screens and in live shows that featured some of America's greatest entertainers.

Black citizens could attend some large white theaters in those days, but they had to sit in cramped upper balconies where their knees touched the seats in front of them and where they had to enter via metal fire escapes.

But at the legendary black Georgia theaters, including the Ritz in Thomasville; the Liberty in Columbus; the Morton in Athens; the Lenox in Augusta; and the Douglass in Macon, black citizens could proudly enter through the main front doors and take whatever seats were available, or those indicated by their tickets.

The Douglass is a typical example of those great theaters, showcasing the early musical talents of Macon residents Little Richard Penniman, Otis Redding Jr., and James Brown, as well as great performances by such legendary

Douglass Theatre is located at 355 Martin Luther King Jr. Boulevard, in Macon; visit douglasstheatre .org.

blues and jazz artists as Ma Rainey, Bessie Smith, Ida Cox, Cab Calloway, and Duke Ellington.

All of that happened because of the vision and drive of Charles Henry Douglass, born on February 17, 1870, the son of a former slave. Douglass had a talent for business, and early in his career operated the Ocmulgee Park Theatre (1904–1906); established the Colonial Hotel; and organized and managed the Florida Blossom Minstrels and Comedy Company.

He opened the original Douglass Theatre in 1912 in an existing structure at 363 Broadway, offering vaudeville acts and other live entertainment, supplemented by silent pictures. He opened the New Douglass Theatre in 1921, with its 750 to 800 seats at 355-359 Broadway (later named Martin Luther King Jr. Boulevard), next to the Douglass Hotel.

After Douglass died in 1940, his wife Fannie and sons Charles Henry and Peter kept the theater going until it finally closed in 1973. The city of Macon became the owner of the Douglass in 1978 saving its unique history.

ELBERTON'S STONEHENGE

It was strange enough in March of 1980 when U.S. Representative D. Douglas Barnard Jr. pulled off a sheet of black plastic on a hill 7 miles north of Elberton to unveil an unusual, Stonehenge-like monument that has since become known as the "Georgia Guidestones." But it was even more bizarre when the supposed true story of the guidestones emerged: A mysterious stranger in his fifties walked into the office of Joe Fendley Sr., president of Elberton Granite Finishing Company, in June of 1979. The man, who spoke with a Midwestern accent and identified himself as Robert C. Christian, had a unique request.

According to Fendley, Christian wanted to create a massive monument to call for world conservation, and to "herald the coming of an age of reason." He even had the money to deposit in an Elberton bank to finance the project. Christian supposedly showed up just one more time in Fendley's office, carrying a shoe box that contained a rough-looking model of what he wanted built.

The Georgia Guidestones that were eventually created consist of six main

Two good Web sites to visit are thegeorgiaguide stones.com and http://mikerault .blogspot.com /2008_10_01 _archive.html.

stones that weigh a total of 237,746 pounds, or about 107 tons. Engraved on the four upright main stones are ten guidelines of advice on how to live a better life, in eight major languages: English, Russian, Mandarin Chinese, Arabic, classical Hebrew, Swahili, Hindu, and Spanish. There are also four base support stones, a capstone, and a center base support stone, all weighing incredible amounts. In addition, there are holes and slots drilled in the Guidestones to align with the North Star and the midsummer and winter solstices, along with a sundial.

Thousands of visitors have found their way to the Guidestones on the edge of the small Georgia town. Some believe the story and others don't, including the former congressman who unveiled the monument. On the day of the unveiling, Barnard felt like he was being drawn into some sort of a joke or hoax.

"I felt very uncomfortable, frankly," Barnard later said. "I just didn't understand it. I can't remember what I said. I must have been ad-libbing really well that day, but it really was something else."

MANTENER LA HUMANIDAD A MENOS
DE 500.000.000
EN EQUILIBRIO PERPETUO CON LA
NATURALEZA
GUIAR SABIAMENTE A LA REPRODUCCION
MEJORANDO LA CONDICION Y
DIVERSIDAD DE LA HUMANIDAD
UNIR LA HUMANIDAD CON UNA NUEVA
LENGUA VIVIENTE
GOBERNAR LA PASION-LA FE-LA
TRADICION
A TODAS LAS COSAS
CON LA RAZON TEMPLADA
PROTEGER A LOS PUEBLOS Y NACIONES
CON LEYES IMPARCIALES Y
TRIBUNALES JUSTOS
PERMITIR A TODAS LAS NACIONES QUE
SE GOBIERNEN INTERNAMENTE
RESOLVIENDO LAS DISPUTAS EXTERNAS
EN UN TRIBUNAL MUNDIAL
EVITAR LEYES MEZQUINAS Y
FUNCIONARIOS INUTILES
BALANCEAR LOS DERECHOS PERSONALES
CON LAS OBLIGACIONES SOCIALES
VALORAR LA VERDAD-LA BELLEZA
EL AMOR
BUSCANDO LA HARMONIA CON EL
INFINITO
NO SER UN CANCRO EN LA TIERRA
DEJARLE ESPACIO A LA NATURALEZA
DEJARLE ESPACIO A LA NATURALEZA

FDR'S LITTLE WHITE HOUSE

It is a bit ironic that Eleanor Roosevelt was glad her husband, U.S. president Franklin Delano Roosevelt, had decided to make another trip south in late March of 1945 to his "Little White House" in Warm Springs, Georgia, near the Alabama state line. She knew his western Georgia retreat near Columbus usually improved his spirits along with his health. She didn't know, however, that he once again would be meeting with his alleged mistress and former secretary, Lucy Page Mercer Rutherfurd.

Roosevelt had been going to Warm Springs since 1924, in hopes that the warm buoyant water would improve his infantile paralysis that had developed three years earlier. He loved being with fellow patients and local residents who treated him with affection and great respect. That led him to build his cottage, which became known as the Little White House, in 1932, when he was serving as governor of New York.

On April 12, 1945, FDR was posing for an oil portrait in the living room of the Little White House. The portrait

For more information about the Little White House, visit www.gastateparks.org/LittleWhite, and for more about Lucy Page Mercer Rutherfurd, visit http://en.wikipedia.org/wiki/Lucy_Page_Mercer_Rutherfurd or www.findagrave.com/cgi-bin/fg.cgi?page=gr&GRid=8434159. And for more about the Unfinished Portrait, visit www.amazon.com/FDRs-Unfinished-Portrait-Elizabeth-Shoumatoff/dp/0822936593.

was being painted by Russian-born artist Elizabeth Shoumatoff, who had been introduced to FDR by Rutherfurd. FDR was about to be served lunch when he suffered a massive cerebral hemorrhage. The president was carried by some men to his tiny, pine-paneled bedroom with its single bed.

Rutherfurd realized that reporters and FDR's family, including his wife, Eleanor, would most likely be descending on the small cottage very soon. She told Shoumatoff that they had to get to Rutherfurd's home in Aiken, South Carolina, before nightfall. So the *Unfinished Portrait*, as it is now known worldwide, was placed into Shoumatoff's car and Shoumatoff, Rutherfurd, and Shoumatoff's photographer, Nicholas Robbins, headed across Georgia, bound for Aiken.

They stopped in a nearby town where they learned that FDR had died. Shoumatoff would carry the portrait with her to her home in New York, and, in time, would donate the unfinished portrait to the Little White House, where it now remains on public display.

FILMING IN GEORGIA

If this stately courthouse looks familiar, you may have seen it in several of the major movies filmed in the tiny town of Crawfordville, located in central Georgia just north of Interstate 20.

Dennis Hopper, Ed Harris, Sada Thompson, Neil Patrick Harris, Reese Witherspoon, Bill Pullman, Barnard Hughes, Robert Duvall, Sissy Spacek, Kristy McNichol, and many other stars have filmed scenes within a short distance of this Taliaferro County courthouse.

Since the turn of the twentieth century, Georgia has been a popular destination for movie and television producers. By the late 1890s, crowds were flocking to vaudeville and opera houses to see Thomas Edison's kinetoscope- and projectoscope-filmed creations. Residents of Augusta in February of 1913 were watching Edison's movies shown in "natural colors" in the Grand Opera House, followed by "talking pictures" in the same theater in October.

Even more amazing, battle scenes for the original silent version of *The Littlest Rebel* were being filmed on the edge of Augusta in May of 1914, by the Pho-

Among the many television series that have used Georgia as a film location are Roots, I'll Fly Away, *and* In The Heat of the Night.

toplay Co. of New York. It starred silent Western cowboys William and Dustin Farnum.

Several more movies were shot in Augusta, including the courthouse scene for *Charity* (1916), which starred Linda Arvidson, estranged wife of legendary director D. W. Griffith.

Oddly, none of the classic Georgia-located movie *Gone with the Wind* was filmed in the Peach State. Neither was baseball player Ty Cobb's short silent film, *Somewhere in Georgia* (1917), which was actually filmed in New York.

But Susan Hayward did come to Georgia in 1950 to film *I'd Climb the Highest Mountain* around Dawsonville and Cleveland, in the north-central Georgia counties of White and Habersham. Gregory Peck, Robert Mitchum, and Polly Bergen also went to Savannah in 1961 to film *Cape Fear*.

Dozens of movies have been filmed in the state, including *Smokey and the Bandit, The Longest Yard, Midnight in the Garden of Good and Evil, Forrest Gump, Glory, My Cousin Vinny, Fried Green Tomatoes, Driving Miss Daisy, Drumline, The Blind Side,* and more.

FORSYTH PARK FOUNTAIN

One of the most photographed objects in Georgia is the European-style fountain in Savannah's Forsyth Park.

Historian and prominent Savannah resident William Brown Hodgson, who married into the wealthy Telfair family in the 1840s, proposed that city officials develop ten wooded acres into the city's first recreational park. The park was named for John Forsyth, who had served as attorney general and governor of Georgia, as well as representing Georgia in the United States House of Representatives and Senate.

From 1819 to 1823, Forsyth also served as the United States minister to Spain. He negotiated the treaty that annexed Florida from Spain. President Andrew Jackson appointed Forsyth as the U.S. Secretary of State, a post not held again by a Georgian until Dean Rusk in 1961.

Forsyth died in 1841 in Washington, D.C., and was buried in the Congressional Cemetery. Both the city of Forsyth in Georgia and the county of Forsyth are named for him.

Possibly even more interesting,

Among the monuments in Forsyth Park is a bust of Confederate major general Lafayette McLaws, who became a tax collector for the IRS after the war, serving briefly as Savannah's postmaster.

Forsyth was one of two sons of Robert Forsyth, who in 1794 became the first federal law enforcement officer killed in the line of duty. Robert Forsyth had been appointed by U.S. president George Washington as one of the thirteen original United States marshals.

Robert Forsyth, who was forty, was shot and killed by former Methodist preacher Beverly Allen when Forsyth was trying to serve court papers on Allen. Allen twice escaped from jails and supposedly fled to Texas, never serving time for his crime.

The elaborate fountain in Forsyth Park was added in 1854. It is believed to be inspired by a fountain at the Place de la Concorde in Paris, France, which seems logical, since William Brown Hodgson met Margaret Telfair in Paris in 1841, the same year that John Forsyth died.

Over the years, many improvements have been made to the fountain, including renovations to the four tritons (half man, half sea serpent) and the robed female figure, and the addition of four spouting swans and underwater lighting.

GEORGIA-INSPIRED SONGS

Anglican evangelist and founder of Methodism John Wesley and his brother, Charles, could probably be regarded as the first published songwriters in Georgia. The brothers wrote literally thousands of hymns, including the popular classics "Hark! The Herald Angels Sing" and "Christ the Lord Is Risen Today."

The brothers were on their way to Savannah to minister in the new colony at the request of Georgia founder and British general, James Oglethorpe, who had settled Savannah in 1733. During the voyage, the brothers were quite impressed with Moravians on board, who were singing German hymns. They immediately set about having their own hymnbook printed for the Anglican services they would hold in Savannah. Their first collection of English psalms, hymns, and translated German hymns used in Savannah was printed in nearby Charleston, South Carolina, with the cover reading, "Collection of Psalms and Hymns, CHARLES-TOWN, Printed by Lewis Timothy, 1737."

By the late 1700s, Savannah and the Georgia capital of Augusta were staging formal concerts, with those

The Georgia Music Hall of Fame in Macon at georgiamusic .org provides a lot of information about the state's musicians. More about the Wesley brothers can be found at the informative site, gbgm-umc .org/umhistory/ wesley/.

two cities and Charleston forming an entertainment-circuit triangle targeted by professional singers and musicians from major cities in the Northeast. This would lead to more songs being composed in the South.

During the Civil War, Augusta was home to many sheet-music printing companies that churned out patriotic songs about the Great South.

The creation of the recording industry led to Georgia studios being established and international hit recordings being made by producers like Atlanta's Bill Lowery. He and native Georgian Ray Charles would become the first two inductees into the Georgia Music Hall of Fame in 1979. The city of Macon was selected as the site for the Georgia Music Hall of Fame building, which opened on September 21, 1996.

Many songs have "Georgia" in their titles, with some of the most popular being "Georgia On My Mind" (the official state song), "The Midnight Train to Georgia," "Sweet Georgia Brown," "Rainy Night in Georgia," and, of course, the Civil War classic, "Marching through Georgia."

GEORGIA'S CAPITAL BEFORE ATLANTA

Many people erroneously believe that Atlanta rather than Milledgeville was the capital of Georgia during the War Between the States, because Atlanta was featured as a major city in Margaret Mitchell's *Gone with the Wind*.

Many others have no clue that the early 1800s Old State Capitol building that still exists in Milledgeville, with its pointed, arched windows and battlements, is one of America's first public buildings constructed in Gothic Revival style.

Following the Revolutionary War, the Georgia General Assembly made the town of Augusta the capital of Georgia for ten years, and then moved it westward to Louisville in 1796. Then in 1804, the state legislature voted to move it still westward to the newly created town of Milledgeville, named for then U.S. senator John Milledge.

The original building was designed simply and enlarged over the course of thirty years, with its north and south wings built in 1828 and 1837 to resemble Gothic churches and castles. Two fires during the ensuing years destroyed much of the building. Restoration in

Georgia's Old Capital Museum, located at 201 East Greene Street on the ground floor of the old statehouse, on the campus of Georgia Military College, is open from 10 a.m. to 4 p.m. Tuesday through Friday, and noon to 4 p.m. on Saturday (oldcapital museum.org). You can also visit the former Georgia Governor's Mansion, 231 West Hancock Street, home to eight state chief executives, open from 10 a.m. to 4 p.m. Tuesday through Saturday and 2 to 4 p.m. on Sunday (gcsu .edu/mansion).

1943 created a new exterior, made to resemble the original building.

For more than sixty years, the state capital building served as the seat of state government, with twenty-one men presiding as Georgia's governor. Their portraits are on the first- and second-floor rotundas. The grounds saw many famous visitors, including the Marquis de LaFayette, entertained there with a barbecue in March of 1825.

One unwelcome visitor was Union general William Tecumseh Sherman, who stopped by in March of 1864 during his infamous "March to the Sea" from Atlanta to Savannah.

One hero of the Yankee invasion was Georgia secretary of state Nathan C. Barnett, who hid the Great Seal under his house and the legislative minutes in a pigpen. The capital of Georgia was moved to Atlanta after the Civil War.

The Old State Capitol building subsequently was used for Baldwin County courtrooms, and to house the county's official records until 1879, when it became part of Middle Georgia Military and Agricultural College, renamed Georgia Military College in 1900.

GOLD-DOMED CAPITOL

There is a 15-foot-tall woman (Miss Freedom) standing on top of Georgia's gold-dome capitol building in Atlanta, and a large replica of the Statue of Liberty on the capitol grounds. Otherwise, the only full-length statue of a woman at the capitol is of Fanny Brown, wife of former governor and Confederate general, John B. Brown. The statues of Governor Brown standing by his seated wife are thought to be among the few husband-and-wife-combination statues in the United States.

Juliette Gordon Low, founder of the Girl Scouts of the USA; Margaret Mitchell, author of *Gone with the Wind*; and Moina Michael, who popularized the use of the red poppy as a universal symbol of tribute and support for military veterans, are honored in the capitol with busts, and the face of pioneer women's suffrage leader Mary Latimer McLendon is depicted on a marble fountain.

There also are some paintings of famous Georgia women including the late black educator Lucy Craft Laney.

The Georgia capitol building itself was designed by Chicago architects

Detailed information about the Georgia state capitol building can be found at sos.ga.gov/archives/state _capitol/.

Franklin Burnham and Willoughby Edbrooke, and completed in 1889. Its exterior structure was built with Indiana limestone, with its interior walls and stairs made of Georgia marble.

Originally the dome was tin-covered, but the gold gilding was added during a 1957 renovation. Citizens of Dahlonega-Lumpkin County, site of the nation's first gold rush, contributed the gold leafing. In August of 1958, a caravan of seven mule-drawn covered wagons made a three-day trip, traveling from Dahlonega in north Georgia to Atlanta, carrying the gold in a chest that was allegedly once owned by U.S. Constitution signer William Few of Georgia.

Unfortunately, that first application of forty-three ounces of twenty-three-karat gold lasted for only about twenty years, due to the fact it was applied in cold weather. That resulted in a second application of sixty ounces of twenty-three-karat gold being added in 1981.

In 1977, the Georgia state capitol building was designated a National Historic Landmark.

GOLFING ON HISTORIC COURSES

Eight of Georgia's state parks and almost all of its major and midsize cities have golf courses. That should tell you something about how much Georgians love the game.

The Georgia cities of Albany, Atlanta, Augusta, Columbus, LaGrange, and Savannah, at this writing, take part in an international effort called The First Tee, which offers children—especially economically disadvantaged children—a chance to be exposed to the game and its positive values. More about The First Tee, founded by the World Golf Foundation in 1997, can be found at thefirsttee.org.

Bobby Jones's home turf was the East Lake Golf Course near downtown Atlanta. It began when the Atlanta Athletic Club was formed in 1898. Its athletic director was John Heisman, the Georgia Tech football coach for whom the famed Heisman Trophy later was named.

The club acquired property known as East Lake in 1904, to be used for a golf course which opened in 1908. There was a six-year-old at the opening reception named Bob Jones, whose

To see Fruitland Manor, now the clubhouse of the Augusta National, visit the official Masters Tournament Web site, masters.com.

father was a member of the club. He grew up playing on the course before becoming the world-famous golfer known as Bobby Jones.

The clubhouse of the Augusta National is probably the most famous clubhouse in the world, but it was almost demolished in the late 1920s. Florida developer "Commodore" J. Perry Stoltz intended to tear down the large 1850s farmhouse, known as Fruitland Manor, once his multistory Augusta Fleetwood hotel was built on the massive Fruitland nurseries property off Washington Road. But Stoltz never got the chance to demolish Prosper Berckmans's farmhouse, because his Augusta hotel was never built, thanks to a major Miami hurricane that wiped out Stoltz's financial empire. The farmhouse and the land were eventually sold to the Fruitland Manor Corporation for $70,000.

And who was revealed on July 15, 1931 to be the one who was backing the Fruitland Manor Corporation? None other than legendary Georgia-born golfer Bobby Jones and his business associates.

GOVERNORS' MANSIONS

As the first resident of the current Georgia governor's mansion, former restaurant owner Lester Maddox raised eyebrows in 1968, even in the "Bible Belt," when he issued a statement saying that "all visitors to the governor's mansion will get a cool sip of cow's milk or a soft drink if they're thirsty, but no alcoholic beverages."

Governors after him, including future president Jimmy Carter, relaxed that directive for social gatherings at the thirty-room Greek Revival–style residence at 391 West Paces Ferry Road Northwest.

Originally governors of Georgia lived in their own homes, as was the case when Augusta was the state capital, from 1785 to 1795. There is a Georgia Historical Commission marker at the corner of East Boundary and Broad Streets in Augusta that notes:

> Here stood the home of Edward Telfair. . . . Telfair became a member of the Continental Congress and was the first governor of Georgia after adoption of the U.S. Constitution. It is believed that as governor he entertained George Washington in his home here in 1791 when Augusta was the state capital.

For a more detailed look at Atlanta, Georgia's governor's mansion, visit mansion.georgia .gov.

From Augusta the capital moved to Louisville and then on to Milledgeville, where a three-story mansion served as the home of eight Georgia governors, until the state capital was moved to Atlanta in 1868. The mansion, which was designed after architect Andrea Palladio's villa in Vicenza, Italy, can be toured today, and was designated a National Historic Landmark in 1973.

It was a large Victorian home at Peachtree and Cain (now International Boulevard) that served as the first official governor's mansion in Atlanta, with seventeen governors and their families using it. The state government in 1925 bought Edwin Ansley's large, granite estate located at The Prado in Ansley Park. Eleven governors and their families used this home until the current governor's mansion was built.

Unique furnishings in the current mansion include an Olympic torch from the 1996 Summer Games in Atlanta, a butternut-paneled library full of books by Georgia authors, and a circa-1810 Paris porcelain vase with twenty-four-karat gold gilt.

JEKYLL ISLAND:
THE MILLIONAIRES' PLAYGROUND

Georgia's beautiful Jekyll Island near Brunswick supposedly was named for Sir Joseph Jekyll, a member of English Parliament and financial supporter of the Georgia colony.

In 1886, the island was turned into a playground and hunting club for millionaires and their families. The Jekyll Club, initially consisting of fifty-three individuals, included such famous Americans as George F. Baker, Marshall Field, John Pierpont Morgan, Joseph Pulitzer, William Rockefeller, and William K. Vanderbilt.

The club members hired Chicago architect Charles A. Alexander to design and build a sixty-room clubhouse, which was finished in late 1887. The clubhouse expanded in 1901 to include an attached annex. Between 1886 and 1928, club members built massive "cottages" to serve as their residences, most of which still exist.

And for their play time, the members constructed a golf course, laid out in 1898, followed by two more courses in 1909. There was also a marina known as

The climactic battle scene for the Civil War movie, Glory, was filmed on the north end of Jekyll Island. More about "Georgia's Jewel" can be found at jekyllisland.com.

the Jekyll Island Wharf, where members who came down on their yachts through the inner-islands waterway could dock; a bowling alley; and a huge indoor tennis court to use when it rained.

One significant meeting took place on the island on November 22, 1910, when U.S. senator Nelson W. Aldrich, chairman of the National Monetary Commission, joined assistant U.S. secretary of the Treasury, A. P. Andrews, and powerful United States banking officials for a major revision of the U.S. banking system, which would eventually become the Federal Reserve.

The increasing development of Florida as a winter resort, the onset of the Great Depression, and the unprotected status of the island from possible enemy attack during World War II spelled the end of the Jekyll Club.

Georgia governor Melvin E. Thompson purchased Jekyll Island in 1947 for the state of Georgia for $675,000.

In 1978, the 240-acre club district was designated a National Historic Landmark.

JULIETTE GORDON LOW

Every year, thousands of Girl Scouts from around the world make a pilgrimage to two places that many Savannahians refer to as "the birthplace" and "the death place."

It was in the two-story mansion at 142 Bull Street that Juliette Magill Kinzie Gordon was born on October 31, 1860. And it was in the two-story, stately house at 329 Abercorn Street on Lafayette Square that widowed Juliette Gordon Low, in her downstairs parlor, founded the Girl Guides of the United States of America on March 12, 1912, and also where she died in her upstairs bedroom on January 17, 1927.

Low came from an incredibly long line of achievers and doers. Her great-grandfather, Major Ambrose Gordon, was in charge of the welcoming party that greeted U.S. president George Washington on the edge of Augusta during his 1791 tour of the Southern states.

Her grandfather, William Washington Gordon, became the first Georgian to graduate from the U.S. Military Academy at West Point, New York. He became mayor of Savannah in 1834, was elected to the Georgia Senate in 1838,

Juliette Gordon Low's grave in Savannah's Laurel Grove Cemetery has become a pilgrimage site for Girl Scouts. She is buried near James Pierpoint, composer of the Christmas song, "Jingle Bells." The house in the right photo is where Juliette founded the Girl Guides of the United States of America and where she died.

and was the first president of Central of Georgia Railroad and Banking Co. Her father, William Washington Gordon II, likewise was a prominent Savannah businessman and civic-minded citizen.

Juliette grew up in the family home on Bull Street, which contains many of her artistic creations. Her adult life was spent in the house on Abercorn Street that she inherited following the death of her alcoholic philandering husband, William Mackay Low.

Low first founded the Girl Guides of the United States of America, which evolved into the Girl Scouts of the USA. Low served as president of the organization from 1912 until her retirement in 1920. She then was given the title "Founder, Girl Scouts of the U.S.A."

Her funeral in January of 1927 was held in Christ Church in downtown Savannah, the same church where she had been baptized and married. She was buried in Laurel Grove Cemetery in her Girl Scouts uniform. Her movement had grown from eighteen original Girl Guides of America to a reported 167,925 Girl Scouts at the time of her death.

MARTHA BERRY COLLEGE

The few words on Martha McChesney Berry's gravestone, located close to the chapel of Martha Berry College near Rome, Georgia, say simply NOT TO BE MINISTERED UNTO BUT TO MINISTER.

That seems an understatement for the daughter of a cotton broker and store owner who was presented to Great Britain's King George V and Queen Mary in England in 1934; named one of "America's Twelve Greatest Women" by *Good Housekeeping* magazine in 1931; had two World War II cargo ships posthumously named in her memory; and whose portrait hangs in the Georgia state capitol's Gallery of Distinguished Georgians.

Although she never attended college herself, Berry was awarded honorary doctorates by eight colleges and universities. Her educational efforts began around 1900, when three north Georgia boys found their way to her log cabin retreat. When she learned they had no Sunday school to attend, she began telling them Bible stories. Other children soon started coming to her cabin.

By 1902, Berry had set aside eighty-three acres, inherited from her father,

The simple Web address berry .edu will take you to the college's official site.

to found the Boys' Industrial School, to teach nearby farm boys about business and mechanical skills in an effort to help them become good farmers. She began including girls at the school in 1909. They took some of the same classes as the boys but also learned homemaking skills. This simple beginning evolved into the founding of a junior college, which eventually grew into a four-year college.

Students in the early years worked at the college in exchange for free tuition and other benefits. They were also required to attend three weekly chapel sessions, and an interdenominational service on Sundays.

Berry received millions of dollars in support from philanthropists Andrew Carnegie and Emily Vanderbilt Hammond, and from automotive pioneer Henry Ford, as well as assistance from U.S. presidents Theodore Roosevelt and Woodrow Wilson. She continued her educational efforts until her death in Atlanta on February 27, 1942.

Martha Berry College now has thirty-five buildings set on more than 28,000 acres. Its campus is said to be the largest in the world.

MOTHER CHURCH OF CIVIL RIGHTS

The last Sunday in June of 1974 didn't seem out of the ordinary as preacher's wife Alberta King sat at the organ of Ebenezer Baptist Church on Auburn Avenue in Atlanta.

She had just started playing "The Lord's Prayer," and the choir had just started singing, when twenty-three-year-old black Ohio student Marcus Wayne Chenault opened fire with a pistol just 3 feet away from the sixty-nine-year-old organist.

He not only killed the organist and a sixty-nine-year-old deacon, but he also shot a sixty-five-year-old woman who would survive. His only reason was that all Christians were his enemies. The story, although horrifying, probably would have rated the inside of many national newspapers had it not been for the fact that the organist was the mother of late civil rights activist, Martin Luther King Jr.

Her oldest son's own funeral had been held in the same brick Atlanta church just six years earlier on April 9, 1968, following his assassination by a white gunman in Memphis, Tennessee.

Rather than Ebenezer being a place of sorrow, however, it is a place of cel-

For more about Ebenezer Baptist Church, visit www.historic ebenezer.org/ Home.html, and for more about the Martin Luther King Jr. National Historic Site, visit www.nps.gov/ malu/index.htm.

ebration and a historic sacred place for both black and white citizens who realize its importance.

"Many of the civil rights movement's mass meetings, rallies, and strategy sessions were held in this historic sanctuary and fellowship hall," said Judy Foot, superintendent of the site. "This is one of the powerful anchors of a world treasure, the Martin Luther King Jr. National Historic Site, which annually welcomes more than 600,000 national and international visitors."

Martin Luther King Jr. was baptized at Ebenezer. In the summer of 1947, at the age of eighteen, he delivered his first prepared sermon in the 1922 Gothic Revival–style church where his father was pastor. He became assistant pastor of Ebenezer in 1948, and co-pastor with his father in 1960, after serving as pastor of Dexter Baptist Church in Montgomery, Alabama.

By the time of King's assassination, the congregation had moved across the street to the New Ebenezer Baptist Church. But, as a "farewell to his spiritual home," the funeral was held at the old Ebenezer Baptist.

OCMULGEE INDIAN MOUNDS

In 1933, Macon-area citizens became alarmed at the lack of respect being shown to the ancient Indian mounds outside their city. Much of the dirt from one mound was used to fill a street, and motorcycle hill-climbers were tearing up the slopes and summit of the Great Temple Mound.

Citizen activists appealed to the Smithsonian Institution for help, which led to Dr. Arthur Kelly's arrival in Macon. The archaeological treasures found by Kelly and his assistants prompted the U.S. Congress in 1934 to establish a 2,000-acre Ocmulgee National Park, and in 1936, to President Franklin D. Roosevelt signing a proclamation establishing the Ocmulgee National Monument.

The site consists of a large temple mound rising some 45 feet high, offering a great view of the Ocmulgee River, a smaller temple mound, and other formations, all believed to have been constructed around A.D. 900–950 during the Early Mississippian Period. Other significant Native American mound formations in Georgia include:

Etowah Mounds: Located on the banks of the Etowah River in northeast

The Ocmulgee Indian Mounds are located beside the Ocmulgee River southeast of Macon, off Interstate 16, on Emery Highway (also U.S. Highway 80).

Georgia, near Cartersville, 5 miles southwest of Interstate 75, this fifty-four-acre state park, containing six earthen mounds believed to date from A.D. 1000 to A.D. 1550, is regarded as the most intact Mississippian Culture site in the southeastern United States.

The largest of the mounds is the 63-foot flat-topped knoll. Excavations of the site indicate Indian nobility may have been buried in elaborate costumes with items for the afterlife, much like with the Egyptian dead. The Etowah Mounds became a registered National Historic Site in 1964.

Kolomoki Mounds: These are located in southwest Georgia on a tributary of the Chattahoochee River, 6 miles north of Blakely, off U.S. Highway 27. This state park features Georgia's oldest great temple mound, four ceremonial mounds, and two burial mounds. It is believed to have been one of the most populous settlements of very early Native Americans north of Mexico. The highest of the seven mounds is 56 feet. Archaeologists believe the main occupation of Kolomoki dates to the Woodland Period (1000 B.C.– A.D. 900).

FLANNERY O'CONNOR'S ANDALUSIA

To many liberal arts college students, native Georgian Flannery O'Connor is as revered a Southern writer as are William Faulkner, Pat Conroy, Carl Sandburg, Eudora Welty, and Erskine Caldwell. Her short stories and novels are filled with bizarre and quirky Southern characters, born of her creative mind. A Catholic spinster, O'Connor spent the last thirteen years of her life writing on her family's 554-acre farm, Andalusia, on the outskirts of Milledgeville.

O'Connor's literary legacy includes two novels (*Wise Blood* in 1952 and *The Violent Bear It Away* in 1960); two collections of short stories (*A Good Man Is Hard to Find* in 1955, and *Everything that Rises Must Converge,* published posthumously in 1965); a collection of nonfiction (*Mystery and Manners* in 1969, edited by Robert and Sally Fitzgerald); another posthumous publication (*The Complete Stories* in 1971, edited by Robert Giroux); and a large collection of O'Connor's letters (*The Habit of Being* in 1979, edited by Sally Fitzgerald).

In the summer of 1966, yours truly served an internship in the newsroom

Andalusia, 4 miles northwest of Milledgeville on U.S. Highway 441, has been listed on the National Register of Historic Places since 1980. Open for self-guided "walk-in" tours from 10 a.m. to 4 p.m. daily, except Wednesday and Sundays (andalusiafarm .org).

of the *Atlanta Journal* daily newspaper and wrote a feature article about Georgia writers. That led to a phone interview with Regina Cline O'Connor, the author's mother, who was living in Milledgeville. Flannery had died just two years earlier at the age of thirty-nine, on August 3, 1964, from lupus, the debilitating blood disease that had also killed her father, Edward, in 1941.

At the conclusion of the interview, I asked Regina if she'd like to add anything else about her daughter. She immediately replied, "Those who didn't know her really missed something."

Other places associated with O'Connor include the Gordon-Cline family home at 311 West Greene Street in Milledgeville; the house at 207 East Charlton Street in Savannah, where her parents were living when she was born on March 25, 1925 (visit flannery oconnorhome.org); and the Flannery O'Connor Room at Georgia College and State University in Milledgeville, which contains many of her personal items including the typewriter she frequently used.

PEACH-PICKIN' TIME DOWN IN GEORGIA

There's a classic country song performed by pioneer country performers Jimmie Rodgers and Clayton McMichen that goes, "When it's peach-pickin' time down in Georgia, it's gal-pickin' time for me."

The state ranks alongside South Carolina and California as one of the largest-producing peach states, but only Georgia has the words PEACH STATE on its official license plates. And the last county created by the Georgia General Assembly is Peach County, founded in 1924 from parts of Houston and Macon counties.

Peaches are believed to have been first grown in China almost 4,000 years ago. Christopher Columbus brought peach seeds to the New World on his second and third trips, and Franciscan monks introduced them to the Georgia coastal islands of St. Simons and Cumberland around 1571.

Georgia's first Peach Festival was staged in Fort Valley, the county seat of Peach County, in 1986. The event was officially incorporated

The site gapeaches.org will tell you more about the crop that gave Georgia its nickname as the Peach State, and the site peachcounty .net will tell you about one of the few counties in the nation named after a fruit.

in 1988 as the Georgia Peach Festival, Inc. It was conceived by Harold Peavy to promote Peach County and the peach industry.

Georgia peaches are available only sixteen weeks each year, from mid-May to August. Agriculture experts say Georgia has more than 15,000 acres of peach trees, which annually yield more than 1.7 million bushels of peaches. Peach County cultivates more than half of that harvest.

One of the first persons to market peaches commercially was an interesting planter and Jewish Confederate general named Raphael Moses. The South Carolina–born lawyer and his wife, Eliza, owned a plantation near Columbus called Esquiline, named after one of the hills near Rome, Italy. Moses is credited with being the first to ship and sell peaches outside of the South, with his success coming from using champagne baskets rather than pulverized charcoal to help preserve the flavor of the fruit during shipping.

The peach became the official state fruit of Georgia in 1995.

PEANUTS IN THE PEACH STATE

Although people the world over know Georgia for cotton, peaches, Vidalia onions, and watermelons, they rarely think about the state in regard to peanuts. But whenever you spread that peanut butter onto your sandwich, crunchy or smooth, you should be thinking about Georgia as the number-one producer of peanuts in the United States, providing almost half of the U.S. peanut crop each year. Each October, the town of Sylvester, Georgia, lures thousands of visitors to the Georgia Peanut Festival.

Those little brown goobers should already be on your mind, since the most famous peanut farmer in the world is former president James "Jimmy" Earl Carter of the small south Georgia community of Plains. In fact, one of the most unusual tributes to a United States president is the 13-foot-tall statue of a toothy, grinning peanut in front of the Davis E-Z Shop in Plains.

The sculpture of wooden hoops covered with chicken wire, polyurethane, and aluminum foil was created by three Indiana residents—James Kiely, Doyle Kifer, and Loretta Townsend—for

The Georgia Peanut Commission offers good insight into the state's peanut industry at gapeanuts.com. More about the state's most famous peanut farmer, former president Jimmy Carter, can be found at jimmycarter library.org.

a 1976 political visit to Evanston by Jimmy Carter. Afterward, it was transported to Plains, where it was displayed for years on the steps of the Plains train depot. It was later moved to the Davis E-Z Shop, where it has become one of the most photographed things in Plains.

Georgia has more than 2,700 peanut farms, resulting in 1.6 billion pounds of peanuts harvested on nearly 519,000 acres of land.

Here are some things about peanuts that you may not know:

- Peanuts are planted in April or May and harvested in September or October.

- Roughly 50 percent of harvested peanuts are used to make peanut butter.

- One acre of peanuts will make about 30,000 peanut butter sandwiches.

- It takes 772 peanuts to make a 16.3-ounce jar of peanut butter.

- Americans eat about 2.4 million pounds of peanut butter and more than 1 million pounds of roasted peanuts every day.

PROVIDENCE CANYON
AND OTHER NATURAL WONDERS

The 1,109-acre Providence Canyon State Conservation Park near Lumpkin actually includes sixteen canyons, some as deep as 150 feet. The colors of the canyon and its rare plants are some of the features that attract many visitors each year.

Historians and geologists attribute the canyon's formation to poor farming practices of the early 1800s, when much forestland was cleared for farming. The sandy nature of the soil was no match for severe rainstorms.

Many famous people have visited the canyon, including General George C. Patton, while serving as the commander of nearby Fort Benning. His signature is in an early guestbook.

Providence Canyon wasn't on the first known list of Georgia's natural wonders, as compiled by state librarian, Ella May Thornton, for an article that was published in the *Atlanta Georgian* magazine in 1926. But over the years, other lists have been created, and the now generally recognized Seven Natural Wonders of Georgia are:

Lots of good information about Providence Canyon can be found at gastateparks .org/Providence. You can also go to georgia encyclopedia.org and type "natural wonders" into the search window for some great links.

1. **Amicalola Falls** near Dawsonville, Georgia's highest waterfalls with a drop of 729 feet;

2. **Okefenokee Swamp** near the Florida state line, covering about 700 square miles in four counties;

3. **Providence Canyon,** called "Georgia's Little Grand Canyon";

4. **Radium Springs** near Albany, largest natural springs in Georgia, with its waters, consistently at 68 degrees, rushing from the earth at 70,000 gallons per minute;

5. **Stone Mountain** near Atlanta, largest exposed granite in the world, 2 miles long and rising 650 feet above the Piedmont plateau;

6. **Tallulah Gorge** in northeast Georgia, a canyon formation 3 miles long and 1,200 feet deep; and

7. **Warm Springs** near Columbus and Radium Springs, also noted for its warm, healing waters, made internationally famous by polio-stricken U.S. president Franklin D. Roosevelt even before the New Yorker became president.

THE REAL GARDEN OF GOOD AND EVIL

Many fans worldwide know Bonaventure Cemetery as the "Garden of Good and Evil," as it figures so prominently in John Berendt's best-seller, *Midnight in the Garden of Good and Evil,* about gay Savannah antiques dealer James Arthur "Jim" Williams and other real-life quirky Savannah residents.

The truth is, with its beautiful, Spanish moss–covered trees, elaborately carved gravestones, and its location beside the Wilmington River, Bonaventure is far more good than evil. Contrary to widespread belief, neither Savannah antiques dealer Williams nor the gay young man he shot and killed, Danny Lewis Hansford (known in the book and movie as Billy Hanson), are buried in Bonaventure.

Williams is buried in Ramah Church Cemetery in Gordon, Georgia, and Hansford is buried in Greenwich Cemetery in Savannah. And, just for the record, Williams was not found "not guilty" of Hansford's death in a Savannah court, but rather in a court in

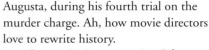

The Bonaventure Historical Society is a nonprofit organization composed of non-salaried volunteers who are dedicated to "the evolution and preservation of the historical significance of Bonaventure Cemetery" (bonaventure historical.org).

Augusta, during his fourth trial on the murder charge. Ah, how movie directors love to rewrite history.

Oscar-winning songwriter Johnny Mercer is buried in Bonaventure. He wrote such classic songs as "Come Rain or Come Shine," "Accentuate the Positive," "Moon River," "The Days of Wine and Roses," "Autumn Leaves," and "Fools Rush In (Where Angels Fear to Tread)."

Other notable Bonaventure residents include Pulitzer Prize–winning poet Conrad Aiken; Jack Leigh, the photographer who took the famous "Bird Girl" statue photo used on the cover of Berendt's best-seller; physician Brodie S. Herndon, said to be the first to perform a caesarean section in the United States; Alexander Lawton, who served as president of the American Bar Association; Marie Scudder Myrick, said to be the first woman in the South to own a daily newspaper (*Americus Times-Recorder*); and Edward Telfair, the first governor elected under the constitution of Georgia.

RECYCLING OLD GEORGIA BUILDINGS

Unfortunately, many of Georgia's great and historic buildings with their unique designs have been lost to disasters such as fires or earthquakes, or have been demolished for newer structures. Many, however, have been saved by visionaries who renovate them for uses other than their original purpose.

One is the Madison-Morgan [County] Cultural Center on South Main Street in the central Georgia town named after President James Madison. The Romanesque Revival–style, redbrick building was constructed in 1895 as one of the first brick schools in the South that divided students into grades.

By the late 1950s, the number of Madison students had outgrown the building, and there actually was talk of tearing the structure down. But three civic-minded men—Robert Turnell, Kay Tipton, and Joe Bell—organized the Morgan County Foundation, Inc., to secure the building and make it available to the public.

The building, which reopened in July 1976, now contains a museum and art galleries, as well as a 397-seat the-

To learn more about the great work being done by The Georgia Trust in saving old buildings, visit georgiatrust.org. The Madison-Morgan Cultural Center (opposite-page photo) is a good example of how old structures can be reused.

ater, which has hosted performances by such artists as the Alvin Ailey American Dance Theater, the Royal Shakespeare Company, and the Vienna Boys' Choir.

Madison makes use of other old buildings, including a former funeral home that is now a popular bookstore, and a bank that is now a popular downtown restaurant. Augusta has a former Catholic church turned into a cultural center, and a former 1920s movie theater used as an optometrist's office. Savannah has former downtown residences turned into restaurants, a "ships of the sea" museum, and an art academy. Athens is using a former Coca-Cola building for retail, office, and residential space.

Since 1973, the nonprofit Georgia Trust for Historic Preservation in Atlanta works to find buyers for historic structures and advocates for government funding, tax incentives, and laws that aid in preservation efforts.

Appropriately, the Trust is headquartered in the Rhodes Hall library and museum, originally built in 1904 of Stone Mountain granite as the home of Amos Giles Rhodes.

OTIS REDDING

In 2002, the city of Macon unveiled a bronze statue of soul music superstar Otis Redding Jr., shown sitting by the Ocmulgee River near the Otis Redding Bridge. It was created by Florida sculptors Bradley Cooley and his son, Bradley Cooley Jr. The statue pays homage to Redding, who was living on his 360-acre "Big O" ranch at Round Oak, Georgia, outside Macon, when his private plane crashed into Lake Monona, Michigan, on December 10, 1967.

It also pays homage to his posthumous international hit single, "(Sitting on) The Dock of the Bay," which Redding began writing on a houseboat in Sausalito, California, and which he recorded in Memphis, Tennessee, the month before his crash.

Redding's big break came at age seventeen when he won The Teenage Party talent show at Macon's Douglass Theatre for fifteen consecutive weeks. The Douglass is where Redding would meet his future wife, Zelma Atwood, and where he would hook up with Macon's legendary musician, Johnny Jenkins, who would hire Redding for his band, The Pinetoppers.

The Otis Redding Statue is located in Gateway Park in Macon, where Martin Luther King Jr. Boulevard crosses the Ocmulgee River.

It was with Jenkins that Redding came to record the ballad, "These Arms of Mine," because Jenkins had some leftover recording time at a Memphis studio. That was his first big hit. Others to follow included "(They Call Me) Mr. Pitiful," "Security," "Pain in My Heart," "Respect" (which he wrote, and which was covered by Aretha Franklin), "I've Been Loving You Too Long," his version of the Rolling Stones's "(Can't Get No) Satisfaction," and his duet with Carla Thomas, "Tramp."

This book's author crossed paths with Redding in 1966, backstage at Atlanta's old Municipal Auditorium, just more than a year before his plane crash. The night before, Redding had performed a sold-out "homecoming" show in Macon's Municipal Auditorium, the same building where his funeral would be held.

When I asked him how it felt for a small-town Georgia native to make it really big, he smiled and said, "I'm happy. I've got all I always wanted. I'm grateful to the kids for buying my records. I hope to sing for a while more, and then come back to my Macon ranch."

RIVERS OF GEORGIA

The Sunday magazine staff of the *Atlanta Journal* and the *Atlanta Constitution* in the early 1960s profiled Georgia's largest rivers: Savannah, Ogeechee, Altamaha, St. Mary's, Suwannee, Coosa, Flint, and Chattahoochee. Their stories were compiled into *Georgia Rivers: Articles from the Atlanta Journal and Constitution Magazine* (edited by George Hatcher, Athens: University of Georgia Press, 1962).

Ralph McGill, Pulitzer Prize–winning columnist and publisher of the *Constitution,* not only wrote the foreword but also the profile on the Chattahoochee. He began with these beautifully crafted words:

> Rivers, of course, are the stuff of dreams. A boy stands on the bank of one and watches its movement. Somewhere, he knows, its waters will reach the sea. His imagination is stirred with a dream of ships and travel, of strange, foreign lands, and adventure. An old man, standing beside the flow of a river, sees in it a symbol of eternity—the waters rolling forever toward some unseen end of a journey.

Other enjoyable rivers in the state include the Ochlockonee, Ocmulgee,

To learn how you can save the rivers of your state, see what Georgia's Rivers Alive organization is doing (http:// aesl.ces.uga .edu/aascd/ RiversAlive/).

Oconee, Satilla, Tallapoosa, and the Tennessee.

There is also Moon River in Savannah, made world-famous in the theme song of the 1961 movie, *Breakfast at Tiffany's.* Savannah native Johnny Mercer, whose home overlooked the river, wrote the lyrics, and Henry Mancini wrote the music. The river was originally known as the Back River, but was later renamed Moon River in honor of Mercer.

Fans of the book *Deliverance* by James Dickey (and the hit movie based on the book) are familiar with the Chattooga River in northeast Georgia, which inspired the fictional Cahulawassee River in the book and 1972 movie. The Web site imdb.com reports that within a year of the movie's release, thirty-one people had drowned while attempting to navigate the stretch of river where much of the movie was filmed.

Rivers Alive is one organization devoted to keeping the state's rivers enjoyable for future generations. It's more than 231,000 volunteers who have collected 5.4 million pounds of garbage in 16,000 miles of waterways.

ROCK EAGLE EFFIGY

About 9 miles north of Eatonton, Georgia, just south of Interstate 20, is a large, man-made formation of milky white quartz rocks. It is so large that, standing beside it, you only see a pile of rocks, but from the top of a nearby three-story tower, you can see that the rocks have been placed to form a giant bird.

The breast of the bird, and its highest point, is 10 feet tall. The main body measures 35 feet wide and 102 feet from head to tail. The bird has a wingspan of 120 feet.

According to those who have studied the mysterious object, the Rock Eagle effigy is supposedly the largest stone effigy in the United States.

While no one really knows its background, the best guess seems to be that it was made by Native Americans (most likely Woodland Indians or Lower Creeks) who used it for religious purposes and other ceremonial activities. Estimates vary on its age of construction, from 2,000 to 5,000 years ago.

Visit the Web site lostworlds .org/rock_eagle .html to see a fascinating video of the Rock Eagle historic site.

The site on which the Rock Eagle is located comprises the largest 4-H center in Georgia (rockeagle4h.org), with 1,428 acres of forestland and a 110-acre lake. Georgia's county extension offices provide 4-H programs at Rock Eagle, including summer-camp opportunities.

Former Savannah mayor and historian Charles Colcock Jones Jr. is credited with making the first measurements of the Rock Eagle in 1877. The site became a 4-H center in 1955, and was added in 1978 to the U.S. Department of the Interior's National Register of Historic Places.

Fifteen miles away in Putnam County is another stone effigy known as Rock Hawk, due to the fact that its tail resembles a hawk's instead of an eagle's. This formation also measures about 100 feet from head to tail, but its main body is 75 feet wide, more than double that of the 35-foot-wide eagle. Rock Hawk measures 132 feet from wing tip to wing tip, slightly wider than the Rock Eagle.

ROSES IN THOMASVILLE

Georgia's official state flower is the spring-blooming Cherokee climber rose, cultivated by the Native Americans before the Revolutionary War.

There are many rose societies throughout the state where gardeners are dedicated to the growing of that particular flower and creating new varieties of it, but the city of Thomasville in the southern part of Georgia is particularly known for its annual celebration devoted to roses.

In late April of 2010, the birthplace of Oscar-winning actress Joanne Woodward staged its 89th annual Rose Show & Festival, complete with the 69th annual Civic Garden Club Flower Show (roses, wildflowers, and other horticulture set to the theme of "Let's Go to the Picture Show!"), 62nd rose parade with floats and marching bands, 33rd annual Rose City 10K Run, 32nd annual Children's Rose Bud Parade, featuring hundreds of area children, and 31st annual 1 Mile Run.

To broaden its audience and supporters, the annual Rose Show & Festival has been expanded to include a luncheon featuring an expert on but-

For more about Thomasville's rose growers, visit thomasville rosesociety.org.

terfly gardening, an "art in the park" festival of arts and crafts, a "bark in the park" event for dog lovers, a golf tournament, and a car and truck show.

The city's celebration of roses began when members of a local garden club entered into the State Fair in Macon a cart displaying colorful fruits and vegetables. The garden club won the first-place prize of $25, which prompted club members to start a Thomasville flower show with a focus on roses.

Needing a place to hold it that first year in 1921, they worked out an arrangement with the owner of Neel's department store, located downtown. The rose show caught on immediately, and it has grown every year since (pun intended). The only year it was not held was 1954, due to a hard freeze that killed all the new budding roses.

The 2010 Rose Show & Festival was once again held downtown. After 1924, the show had moved to various locations, including a car dealership, a tobacco warehouse, an airplane hangar, a gymnasium at a veterans' hospital, and the local fairgrounds.

CHEROKEE CHIEF JOHN ROSS

Near the Tennessee and Alabama boundary lines, there is a house believed to be the oldest remaining structure in northwest Georgia. It was the residence of a Scottish American named John Ross, who served as chief of the Cherokee Nation for more than forty years.

The house was built circa 1797 by Ross's maternal grandfather, John McDonald, a native of Scotland. At the age of eighteen, John Ross moved into the house after his part-Cherokee mother, Mollie McDonald Ross, died in 1808. He would have ownership of the house—which at various times served as a post office, country store, and schoolhouse—until 1827, when he sold it to a relative. The house passed through several owners before becoming a public historic site. It is now open June through September for public tours in the small town of Rossville.

Ross, whose father also was born in Scotland, was raised in northwest Georgia, heavily immersed in Cherokee culture but educated by English-speaking people. He became a successful businessman in his twenties, and went on to own a ferryboat business.

More information about John Ross's house, which is open to the public, can be found at roadsidegeorgia.com/site/rosshouse.html.

Because Ross could speak English, he became a translator for Cherokee leaders who traveled to Washington, D.C., to "negotiate" treaties between the federal government and his people. The government bought Cherokee land following the Indian Removal Act, passed by the U.S. Congress in 1830.

Two years earlier, Ross had become the first constitutional principal chief and official leader of the Cherokee Nation.

The federal government by the late 1830s had rounded up Cherokees into relocation camps to move them to Oklahoma. Chief Ross, seeing the hopelessness of the situation, was allowed to organize the roughly 15,000 Cherokees into smaller groups so they could forage for food during their forced journey of more than 2,000 miles.

This action saved many lives, but the winter migration of 1838–39 still resulted in the deaths of about 4,000 Cherokee men, women, and children, including Ross's own wife, Quatie, who gave up her blanket to a sick child.

Ross died in 1866 and was buried in Park Hill, Oklahoma.

SAVANNAH'S
ST. PATRICK'S DAY PARADE

St. Patrick's Day 2010 may have been a "big day for the Irish" in general, but it was an even bigger day for sixty-six-year-old Dennis M. Herb Sr., who had been selected as honorary parade marshal of the city of Savannah's 186th St. Patrick's Day parade.

The 2010 parade, billed as the second largest in the nation next to New York City's, still boasted more than 10,000 participants in spite of drizzling rain. It lasted from about 10:15 a.m., when it began at Abercorn and Hall Streets, to its conclusion just past Chippewa Square at around 2:30 p.m.

Dana Clark Felty, in covering the 2010 celebration for the *Savannah Morning News,* noted that between 300,000 to 700,000 people annually descend upon Savannah for its St. Patrick's Day celebration. A Protestant group known as the Hibernian Society organized Savannah's first St. Patrick's Day parade in 1824, to celebrate Irish culture and raise money for poor Irish immigrants fleeing the Great Famine and settling in Savannah.

The official site of the Savannah parade is savannahsaint patricksday.com.

Felty said that in 1961, the city tried to dye the Savannah River green, like the annual coloring of the Chicago River, but when a line of boats spanning the 600-foot-wide channel each emptied forty-five gallons of green dye, the current swept it out to sea.

One ritual that does remain began in the early 1900s, when Benedictine Catholic school cadets marching in the parade were showered with kisses from St. Vincent girls. Now almost anyone is a target for kissing proponents, including firemen and soldiers.

The city-county government by law does allow anyone older than twenty-one to drink alcoholic beverages publicly along the parade route, in a sixteen-ounce plastic cup or smaller, within the downtown tourist area. That "to-go cup" rule is true 365 days a year in Savannah, but the Savannah-Chatham County Metropolitan Police do not tolerate abuse of that privilege. There were seventy-one people arrested before, during, and after the 2010 parade, mostly for misdemeanors.

SAVANNAH'S WAVING GIRL

Many visitors to Savannah's river-front who see the huge statue of a woman waving a piece of cloth with a collie by her side, erected in 1972, do not realize that the "Waving Girl" was a real person.

In fact, it is estimated that between 1887 and 1931, Florence Margaret Martus waved both day and night to more than 50,000 passenger and freight ships entering or leaving the mouth of the Savannah River, near where it meets the Atlantic Ocean.

No one really knows why she took up this lonely, solitary mission. Some think she was hoping for a lover to return from overseas. Martus herself said that she was simply waving hello to seafarers coming to the end of their journeys and waving good-bye to those starting new ones.

Martus lived with her brother, George, on Elba Island, and helped him take care of Elba and Cockspur Island lighthouses.

One morning at about 3:00 a.m., Florence spotted flames on the river

The statue of the waving girl and her collie was created by Vienna-born sculptor Felix de Weldon, who also created the famous statue in Washington, D.C., of the American flag being raised by U.S. Marines on Iwo Jima during World War II.

and realized it was the U.S. government dredge boat that helped keep the Savannah River channel clear for boats. She alerted her brother, and they leapt into their small boat and managed to save more than thirty men. Not long afterward, she and her brother saved twelve young people of Savannah, members of the Fun and Frolic Club, rescuing them from a burning launch that was being swept out to sea.

For forty-four years, she waved a white flag during the day and a lantern at night. She apparently trained her dogs to wake her up at night when ships were approaching.

The end of her mission in life came when her brother retired from the Lighthouse Service. Her last wave came on June 1, 1931. Florence Martus died in a Savannah hospital at the age of seventy-four on February 8, 1943. Her beloved brother, George, had died just a few years earlier. It is said that in deep respect, tugboats and other ships in port on the Savannah River lowered their flags to half-mast.

FLORENCE MARTUS
1869 — 1943
SAVANNAH'S WAVING GIRL

ERECTED BY THE ALTRUSA CLUB
SAVANNAH, GEORGIA   1971

SEEDS FROM THE SOWER

Motorists who exit Interstate 16 and travel through Metter on Georgia Highway 121 often are startled to see a large glass chapel on the edge of town that boasts "Everything's Better in Metter."

One good reason for why it's better is due to a former dance-band leader named Michael Guido, who made Metter the headquarters of his international radio, television, and print ministry based on inspirational Christian stories, called Seeds from the Sower.

By the time he died on February 21, 2009, at the age of ninety-four, Guido had recorded his Seeds from the Sower devotional message programs from Metter for more than fifty years, airing on more than 400 radio stations and more than 90 television stations. His print ministry was mailing more than 1.5 million pieces of literature annually, and his column, also called "Seeds from the Sower," was being published in more than 1,300 weekly and daily newspapers.

In his 1990 autobiography, *Seeds from the Sower: The Michael and Audrey Guido Story,* he wrote about leading a jazz dance band in nightclubs and the-

Learn more about Michael Guido's worldwide ministry at the-sower.org. Don't forget the hyphen, or you'll get another Web site.

aters before turning to gospel music. He began his ministry in his native Ohio after attending a Baptist revival service at nineteen, where he was touched by the message of a loving God.

Eventually, he moved his ministry to the Deep South where he would meet his Metter-reared wife, Audrey, who used magic tricks to hold young people's attention while delivering Christian messages.

Unlike many evangelists, the Guidos never asked for money directly. They would let their needs be known through prayer boards and other indirect means, and usually what they needed would be provided.

In 1992, at the suggestion of floral designer Eddie Smith, Guido began decorating his landscaped gardens during December with white lights, red ribbons, wreaths, and both secular and non-secular Christmas displays. The first event used 36,000 lights and lured several hundred visitors. Fifteen years later, the gardens were being decorated with more than two million lights and luring 40,000 to 60,000 people each December.

The ministry is continued today by Guido's brother, Larry.

SPRINGER OPERA HOUSE

The year 1876 was a major theatrical one for Georgia, as the legendary tragedian Edwin Booth headed south for a series of productions. Booth had only resumed his acting career ten years earlier, in the wake of his brother, John Wilkes Booth, murdering President Abraham Lincoln.

For his return to the stage in 1866, Edwin Booth had chosen the title role in Shakespeare's tragedy *Hamlet,* which had earned him many editorial accolades in the past. And so it was that he repeated this role at Girardey's Opera House in Augusta, Georgia, on January 28, 1876, and at the Springer Opera House in Columbus a few days later, on February 15.

Girardey's Opera House in Augusta no longer exists, but the Springer, with its magnificent interior, still offers regular productions.

Francis Joseph Springer from the Alsace region of eastern France opened his opera house, with its 40-foot-deep stage, on February 27, 1871. Perhaps the Chattahoochee River reminded the successful grocer of the Rhine River in his native land. Perhaps he missed the

For more about the Springer Opera House in Columbus, visit www.springeroperahouse.org/plaintext/home/home.aspx.

splendor of the great European theaters. Either way, he was determined to construct his own theatrical palace.

The stage of the Springer Opera House hosted such illustrious talents as Oscar Wilde, Ethel Barrymore, Martha Graham, Agnes DeMille, Buffalo Bill Cody, General Tom Thumb, Will Rogers, John Philip Sousa, and Columbus's own hometown stars: black Georgia piano prodigy "Blind Tom" Bethune, and blues pioneer Gertrude "Ma" Rainey.

As with other great theaters, the invention and subsequent popularity of silent and talking films led to the demise of the Springer, which closed in 1959. It might have gone the route of Girardey's Opera House had not the Columbus Little Theater Opera House Trustees been formed in 1964 to prevent its destruction. The Springer reopened in late 1965, with The Little Theater's musical production of *St. Elmo,* based upon the novel by Columbus-born author Augusta Evans Wilson.

The Springer was added to the National Register of Historic Places in 1970 and named a National Historic Landmark in 1978.

STONE MOUNTAIN

Granite quarried from Stone Mountain has been used in the construction of the Panama Canal locks, the United States Capitol building in Washington, D.C., and the Imperial Hotel in Tokyo, Japan.

As early as 1909, Helen Plane believed that the soldiers of the Confederacy—including her husband, who had fought with General Robert E. Lee and died at Gettysburg—should be honored with a carving on the side of the largest exposed granite in the world, located 10 miles east of Atlanta.

Her initial idea was just to honor Lee, but the original sculptor, Gutzon Borglum, who was brought on board about 1915, suggested other figures should be added. Those figures eventually became Confederate president Jefferson Davis and generals Robert E. Lee and Thomas "Stonewall" Jackson. Delays led Borglum to begin another project that would become his most famous: four United States presidents on the side of Mount Rushmore in South Dakota.

One notable visitor during the Borglum period of the project was future *Gone with the Wind* novelist Peggy

Visit stone mountainpark .com or http:// ngeorgia.com/ ang/Stone_ Mountain for more information.

Mitchell, who then was a reporter for the *Atlanta Journal* Sunday magazine.

New York sculptor Augustus Lukeman took over the project in 1926, with the supervision of carvers George Weiblen and Theodore Bottinelli. Work was halted again around 1928, and the project remained dormant for about thirty years.

In 1958, the state of Georgia purchased the privately owned mountain, and work on the carvings resumed in the 1960s. This led to the addition of other attractions, including a reconstructed antebellum plantation, a skylift, a waterside complex, and a thirty-six-hole golf course. Actress Thelma "Butterfly" McQueen, who portrayed the slave girl Prissy in the movie version of *Gone with the Wind,* was hired from 1963 to 1965 to be the hostess at the plantation house, greeting visitors, signing autographs, and posing for photos.

In May of 1970, Vice President Spiro Agnew substituted for the originally scheduled President Richard Nixon, dedicating the carving, which was considered officially complete in 1972.

SWAMPWISE OKEFENOKEE JOE

Millions worldwide know about south Georgia's Okefenokee Swamp with its 438,000 acres because of the (1948–1975) daily comic strip *Pogo,* created by Walt Kelly, and through the "swampwise" teachings of a unique person known as Okefenokee Joe.

Joe was the swamp's animal curator and only resident for eight years, living on the northern edge of Cowhouse Island. His video, *Know Your Snakes: Venomous Snakes of the Southeastern United States,* has been used as a teaching tool in hundreds of schools, and his highly rated Georgia PBS television specials have aired many times over the state's nine PBS TV stations, including *Okefenokee Joe and Friends, The Joy of Snakes,* and *Swampwise,* which won an Emmy Award.

For two decades, Joe has made more than 250 appearances a year at schools, colleges, state fairs, Native American gatherings, and conservancy areas, combining his musical talents with live snake demonstrations.

In the early 1950s and '60s, he was known by his real name of Dick Flood,

Okefenokeejoe .com is Dick Flood's official Web site.

and was a popular country music singer and songwriter who recorded for Monument Records, made guest appearances on the Grand Ole Opry, and performed for American soldiers throughout the Far East, including Vietnam.

His song, "Trouble's Back in Town," was a number-one hit single for the Grand Ole Opry duo, the Wilburn Brothers, and was used as the theme song for their syndicated television show.

Flood's second divorce led him to camp for four months in the Florida Everglades before becoming animal curator at the Okefenokee Swamp. The breakup of his third marriage led him to move in with close friends Linda and Bill Macky, who welcomed him to their Augusta-area home. He since has moved to his own house in a rural area near Augusta. "It's hard for me to explain my life because what I'm doing now is what I've always been trained to do all these years," he said. "I call it God's work. But, if you're going to do what I do, you've got to be prepared to be poor, even though I'm still rich in other ways."

TYBEE LIGHTHOUSE

It was a historic occasion when George Jackson died in 1948. He was the last head keeper of the Tybee Lighthouse. The United States Coast Guard already had taken over the lighthouse in 1939, but Jackson was allowed to remain at the lighthouse as head keeper until his death.

Since 1987, the maintenance and usage of the lighthouse has been the joint responsibility of the city of Tybee and the Tybee Island Historical Society.

The Tybee lighthouse is the oldest and tallest active lighthouse in Georgia, with hundreds of visitors each year climbing its 178 steps for a great view of where the mouth of the Savannah River opens into the Atlantic Ocean.

Beginning in the late 1800s, when the third Tybee lighthouse in the area was erected, three lighthouse keepers were needed to operate, in shifts, what was viewed as a major aid to shipping navigation. The advent of electricity, which replaced the lighthouse's frequently needed fuel of kerosene, reduced the staffing needs to just one person in 1933.

Detailed information about Georgia's oldest "light station" can be found at tybeelighthouse .org.

In addition to the historic Tybee lighthouse, visitors to the area can see within 15 miles:

- **Fort Screven:** Located just a few yards from the Tybee lighthouse, and featuring gun batteries, this fort was built on the island in 1885. Named for Revolutionary War hero General Joseph Screven, the fort is part private residence and part museum, and showcases 400 years' worth of the area's history.

- **Fort Pulaski:** Named for Revolutionary War hero and Polish count, Kazimierz Pulaski, this fort was completed in 1847, after eighteen years of construction, with brick walls 11 feet thick. One of its engineers was Second Lieutenant Robert E. Lee.

- **John Wesley Prayer Site:** Near the visitor information center at Fort Pulaski is a Georgia Historical Commission marker that says, "On February 6, 1736, John Wesley, the founder of Methodism, landed at Peeper (now Cockspur) Island near here, and there preached to his fellow voyagers his first sermon on American soil."

THE VARSITY: WORLD'S LARGEST DRIVE-IN RESTAURANT

It's a good thing Georgia Tech dropout Frank Gordy changed the name of his restaurant from the Yellow Jacket to The Varsity, or else the branch he opened in Athens probably would not have been popular with University of Georgia students in that town.

Gordy dropped out of the Georgia Institute of Technology in 1925, and started his Yellow Jacket restaurant three years later at the corner of Luckie Street and Hemphill Avenue, with the goal of providing Georgia Tech students some-place to eat other than the cafeteria. The Thomaston, Georgia, native was twenty-one when he started his venture with a $2,000 nest egg. Two years later he changed the name of his place to The Varsity and moved it to North Avenue and Spring Street, to make it larger. That location today can accommodate 600 vehicles outside and more than 800 people inside.

The home page of thevarsity.com site notes that the restaurant makes from scratch daily "2 miles of hot dogs, a ton of onions, 2,500 pounds of potatoes, 5,000 fried apple, peach, and other

The Web site for the world's largest drive-in restaurant is thevarsity.com.

kinds of fried pies, and 300 gallons of chili." It also sells more Atlanta-created Coca-Cola each year than any other single location in the world.

Gordy branched out to Athens and opened a Varsity downtown in 1932, and a larger one on the west side of Athens in 1963. The downtown location was closed in 1978. Other branches exist, including a mini Varsity at Reinhardt University in Waleska, Georgia, where Gordy started his higher education and met his wife, Evelyn, in 1924.

Many celebrities have been spotted mingling with regular Varsity customers, including U.S. presidents Jimmy Carter, George H. Bush, and Bill Clinton during their terms in office.

The restaurant was featured in the movie *We Are Marshall,* and one of The Varsity's carhops was future television and movie comedian, Nipsey Russell.

By 1979, the restaurants started by college dropout Gordy were grossing $6 million per year. He died in June of 1983 and was buried in Atlanta's West-view Cemetery.

WORLD-FAMOUS VIDALIA ONIONS

There may not be many crops that are embargoed for an official shipping date, but that is the case with the world-famous sweet Vidalia onions, officially grown in only 20 of Georgia's 159 counties.

In 1986, the Georgia General Assembly defined the sole production area as all of thirteen counties—Emanuel, Candler, Treutlen, Bulloch, Wheeler, Montgomery, Evans, Tattnall, Toombs, Telfair, Jeff Davis, Appling, and Bacon—and portions of seven others: Jenkins, Screven, Laurens, Dodge, Pierce, Wayne, and Long.

To ensure the best quality and maintain their reputation, approved Vidalia growers each year adhere to the shipping date (usually in April) recommended by the official Vidalia Onion Advisory Panel to the Georgia Department of Agriculture.

In 2010, the Georgia Department of Agriculture registered eighty Vidalia onion growers to harvest the multi-million-dollar crop on 11,600 acres in the twenty-county growing area. There are about twenty seed varieties of onions approved for planting as Vidalias by the

To learn more, visit vidaliaonion festival.com or vidaliaonion.org. You can also visit the Vidalia Onion Museum at 100 Vidalia Sweet Onion Drive in Vidalia.

Georgia Agricultural Commission. Each year the registered growers insert about 70,000 seedlings per acre, by hand, into the unique low-sulphur soil.

The Vidalia onion industry began in the early 1940s, when the state of Georgia built a farmers' market in Vidalia. That's when the word began spreading about "those sweet onions from Vidalia." It didn't hurt that the then-powerful Piggly Wiggly grocery store chain happened to have a distribution center in Vidalia, which led to nationwide Piggy Wiggly and other chain stores stocking the product.

In 1990, the Vidalia onion was designated by the Georgia General Assembly as the "official state vegetable." Vidalia-minded civic groups in 1978 staged the first Vidalia Onion Festival to promote the local cash crop and raise funds for the community. The festival in recent years has drawn an average of 75,000 visitors. The thirty-third annual festival in late April of 2010 offered visitors freshly cooked Vidalia onion rings, an onion-eating contest and onion-cooking demonstrations.

BEAUTIFUL AND DANGEROUS WATERFALLS

The many waterfalls in Georgia attract thousands of visitors every year who enjoy their beauty and soothing sounds. But also almost every year they result in a fatality or two when visitors—seemingly oblivious to their danger—fall on slippery rocks or are swept over the falls by their strong current.

The most tragic incident involving a Georgia waterfall happened at about 1:30 a.m. on November 5, 1977, when 9 inches of rain fell over two days, causing an earthen dam above beautiful Toccoa Falls to break, releasing the water from forty-acre Kelly Barnes Lake, which then poured over the falls toward Toccoa Falls Bible College, a half-mile downstream. It crashed into the men's dormitory, killing three, and proceeded toward a trailer park, where it swept several mobile homes downstream. The total death toll was thirty-nine, including nineteen children and two volunteer firefighters who had been trying to warn residents.

The waterfall at Toccoa plunges 186 feet and is 19 feet taller than Niagara Falls.

Other particularly notable waterfalls in the state include:

The site georgiatrails .com/waterfalls .html offers good links to scenic waterfalls in the state, as does georgia encyclopedia .com/waterfalls. Toccoa Falls is seen in the right photo.

- **Amicalola Falls:** Located in Dawson County near Ellijay and Dahlonega, and near the southern terminus of the Appalachian Trail.

- **Tallulah Gorge:** Tallulah Gorge State Park in northwest Georgia offers five major waterfalls powered by water from the Tallulah River.

- **Anna Ruby Falls:** These spectacular double falls are located near Unicoi State Park, just north of Helen.

- **Duke's Creek Falls:** Bits of gold have been taken from the waters of these falls north of Helen for more than five hundred years.

- **DeSoto Falls:** Near Dahlonega, there are five beautiful falls along the 3-mile section of the DeSoto Falls Trail, ranging from 20 to 200 feet.

- **Dick's Creek Falls:** Many swimming holes are found near this multitiered waterfall near Clayton.

- **Helton Creek Falls:** Located near Vogel State Park not far from Blairs-ville, these two falls are reached by a well-maintained path.

WATSON MILL COVERED BRIDGE

Historians believe that more than 200 covered bridges once existed in Georgia, yet fewer than 15 of those original historic bridges remain today.

One of the best, and considered the longest in the state (229 feet), is the Watson Mill Bridge southeast of Comer, built in 1885 by Washington W. King, son of a freed slave named Horace King.

Horace King was born on September 8, 1807, in the Cheraw district of South Carolina, of African and Native American ancestry. He and his mother were bought by a contractor named Godwin in about 1830 and taken to Columbus, Georgia, after Godwin won the contract to build the first public bridge over the Chattahoochee River.

Between about 1832 and 1846, King and Godwin built wooden bridges, covered and not covered, in South Carolina, Georgia, and Alabama. Godwin helped King secure his freedom in 1846, more than a decade before the Civil War. King would continue to work with Godwin up until Godwin's death in 1859.

King's three sons joined their father in the bridge-building business.

Two good Web sites for Georgia's covered bridges are: www.n-georgia.com/covered bridges.htm and www.dot.state.ga.us/travelingin georgia/covered bridges/Pages/default.aspx.

Two covered bridges in Georgia attributed to him are the Red Oak Creek Bridge in Meriwether County (believed to have been built in the 1840s, and the oldest remaining covered bridge in the state); and a bridge that was built about 1870 that originally existed in Troup County, later moved to Callaway Gardens near Columbus.

Besides the Watson Mill Bridge, other covered bridges in Georgia attributed to Washington King are the Euharlee Covered Bridge, built about 1886 in Bartow County; and a bridge moved to the Stone Mountain Park near Atlanta, built about 1891 and originally located in Clarke County, near Athens.

The Georgia Department of Transportation and the Georgia Historical Society have historical markers at the abovementioned covered bridges, as well as seven others, including the Concord Bridge in Cobb County; Poole's Mill Bridge in Forsyth County; Coheelee Creek Bridge in Early County; Howard's Bridge in Oglethorpe County; Cromer's Mill Bridge in Franklin County; Elder's Mill Bridge in Oconee County; and Stovall Mill Bridge in White County.

WHITE-COLUMNED MANSIONS

Medora Field Perkerson in her book, *White Columns in Georgia* (New York: Holt, Rinehart and Winston, 1952), writes of the "romantic era" in the South's "great heyday" of white-columned mansions. "In that era," she noted, "cotton was truly king, and Southern hospitality required a house large enough to accommodate visiting friends and relatives who might linger for a month or a year or a lifetime."

One of the best-known historic mansions in Georgia is the four-level former residence of Confederate secretary of state Robert Toombs, with its four massive, white, Doric-style Greek columns in Washington, east of Athens. The house was built by Dr. Joel Abbott in 1794, a physician who served in the U.S. Congress from 1817 to 1825. Toombs purchased the house in 1837 and enlarged it, adding the Doric columns, a west wing, and an east wing.

One frequent visitor to the house was Alexander H. Stephens, vice president of the Confederacy, and later, governor of Georgia. The two were such

More about the Robert Toombs house and other historic Georgia mansions can be found by clicking on the "historic sites" link at www.gastate parks.org/ RToombs.

close friends that Stephens, who lived about 15 miles away in Crawfordville, reserved a bedroom on the second floor of his mansion for Toombs, and Toombs reserved a second-floor bedroom in his mansion for Stephens.

Toombs served in the Georgia General Assembly from 1837 to 1843, and helped create the Georgia Supreme Court. He was elected to the U.S. House of Representatives in 1845, and to the U.S. Senate in 1853.

Unlike many other Confederate leaders, Toombs was not captured at the end of the war but managed to flee to Paris, France, where he and his wife lived briefly in exile. His wife returned to America in November of 1866, when she received word of their daughter Sallie's fatal illness. Her husband returned the next year, quietly settling back in Georgia and reopening his law office in his home.

Toombs's close friend Stephens died in 1883, followed the same year by Toombs's wife, Julia. Toombs himself would die two years later in his bedroom, on December 15, 1885.